NEW YORK'S ADIRONDACK PARK

A USER'S GUIDE

© 2013
HUNGRY BEAR PUBLISHING
Publisher: Andy Flynn
40 McClelland St.
Saranac Lake, NY 12983
(518) 891-5559
EMAIL: adkhungrybear@yahoo.com
www.hungrybearpublishing.com

Book design and editing by Andy Flynn

ISBN: 978-0-9857607-2-4

ACKNOWLEDGMENTS
Much of the content in this book was supplied by the Adirondack Forest Preserve Education Partnership, an unincorporated group of partner organizations from the Adirondacks which includes the Adirondack Mountain Club, Wildlife Conservation Society, Adirondack Park Invasive Plant Program, Adirondack Regional Tourism Council, Leading Edge and the New York State Department of Environmental Conservation. The remainder of the content was written by Andy Flynn. Thanks also to the Adirondack Museum for photo use.

COVER PHOTO: A September sunrise on Lake Simond in the town of Tupper Lake. *Photo by Andy Flynn*

Table of Contents

About the Publisher

Andy Flynn is an author, editor and publisher living in Saranac Lake, N.Y. He is the author of the six-volume "Adirondack Attic" book series and "Saranac Lake Winter Carnival Memories" and producer of two shows on North Country Public Radio, "Adirondack Attic" and "New York's Bluegrass Trail." When he's not operating Hungry Bear Publishing with his wife, Dawn, he works full-time as the assistant managing editor at Denton Publications in Elizabethtown. As part of his duties, he is the editor of the North Creek News Enterprise.

Welcome to the Adirondack Park

We understand that "New York's Adirondack Park: A User's Guide" is more information than you need to enjoy the Adirondack Park for a quick stay, but that's the point. We wanted to give the public — residents and visitors — a valuable reference guide that would help them responsibly use the Forest Preserve while giving them informational links to the community assets (the fun stuff), such as attractions, special events and recreational opportunities.

Yet we went further, including some of Andy Flynn's stories from the "Adirondack Attic" book series to help illustrate the "how-to" aspects of using the Forest Preserve and give a much-needed historical perspective. We also wanted to humanize the Park since it's the communities that really make this place so unique.

Overall, we wanted to answer the question, "What is the Adirondack Park?" Using all our resources from government, not-for-profit and historical organizations, we believe we've answered that question. Yet, to really understand the Adirondack Park and all its nuances, you have to live here or visit often. And we hope you do.

About the Park

Founded in 1892 by the New York State Legislature, the Adirondack Park encompasses about 6 million acres in the northern tier of New York state. The Park is highly regarded as a model for park managers throughout the world. It is about the size of Vermont.

Where's the Gate?

The Adirondack Park has no gate. There is no park ranger who opens and closes the entrance each day. Instead, an imaginary "Blue Line" surrounds a vast region that includes wilderness and human communities with about 135,000 residents.

The Adirondack Park is the largest protected area in the lower 48 states. But unlike most state and federal parks, the Adirondack Park is a patchwork of public and private land. Along with stands of old growth pine and primeval wetlands, you'll find 135 communities.

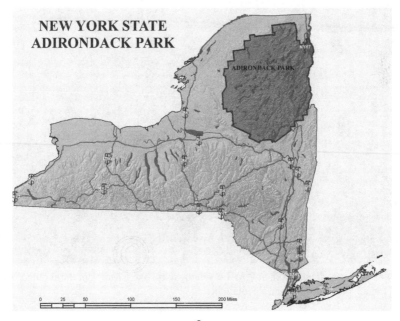

NEW YORK STATE
ADIRONDACK PARK

Who runs the Park?

No single organization oversees the management of the Adirondack Park. Several state agencies work with local governments and not-for-profit groups to manage park lands.

The New York State Adirondack Park Agency oversees state and private land plans for the Park and regulates a permit program intended to protect designated rivers, wetlands and the less-developed forest and open space lands of the Park.

The New York State Department of Environmental Conservation is responsible for stewardship of state-owned public lands in the Park and managing wildlife populations.

Local governments address the day-to-day issues facing counties, towns and villages throughout the Park. Not-for-profit organizations promote special projects ranging from recreation trails to habitat protection and stewardship. Economic development organizations focus on the prosperity of Park communities.

The Blue Line

Locals refer the Adirondack Park boundary as the "Blue Line" because when a commission was set up to explore the possibility of creating the Adirondack Park, it used a blue line as the boundary. The original Adirondack Park boundary was adopted in 1892.

Public and Private Land

According to the Adirondack Park Land Use Classification Statistics, provided by the Adirondack Park Agency in 2011, about 43 percent of the land inside the Park is owned by the state, 51 percent is privately owned, and 6 percent is water. As the state buys more land, those numbers will obviously change.

Key battles were fought here at Fort Ticonderoga on Lake Champlain during the French and Indian War and American Revolution.

Photo by Andy Flynn

ADIRONDACK PARK · INVASIVE PLANT PROGRAM

SINCE 1998

APIPP

Protect Our Adirondack Woods and Waters
PREVENT THE SPREAD OF INVASIVE SPECIES

Invasive plants and animals are not native and pose a major threat to recreation, forestry, fisheries, human health, agriculture, industry and the environment.

While many invasive species can't move far on their own, they can jump hundreds of miles when assisted by humans.

HELP STOP THE SPREAD OF INVASIVES
Here's how:

- Clean, drain and dry waders, gear, boats and trailers between waterways
- Never transport fish between waterways; dispose of unwanted bait in the trash
- Don't move firewood, buy it where you burn it
- Plant only non-invasive plants in gardens and ornamental ponds

Protect your favorite places.

www.adkinvasives.com

Forest Preserve Centennial Knife

ANDY FLYNN

It wouldn't surprise me if a man, outfitted in dark blue jeans, a red-and-black checkered L.L. Bean shirt and a harmless-looking pocket knife hooked onto his shiny leather belt, walked up to me today and asked, in a New York City accent, "What time does the park close?" He, of course, would be referring to the Adirondack Park.

While Adirondack residents may suffer violent chest pains during subsequent laughing fits — before answering, "The park is always open, duh!" — they could save money on pain medication by putting themselves in this guy's shoes for a moment and answering the question tactfully. I know it's not always easy, and some blunt people simply can't restrain themselves, but tourism offices throughout the Adirondacks get this kind of question every day. As the senior public information specialist at the Adirondack Park Agency Visitor Interpretive Center in Paul Smiths from 2001 to 2009, I answered questions like this on the phone all the time. "Can I bring my dog to the park?" Yes, we got that one a lot.

The best question I got was from Montreal, a person asking, "Where is the Adirondack Park located inside the village of Lake Placid?" I had to explain nicely that the village of Lake Placid is actually inside the Adirondack Park.

What's obvious to us — that National Park Service rangers are not collecting money in blue toll booths at several Adirondack Park gates and that we're open 24 hours a day, seven days a week, 365 days a year — may not be obvious to visitors from New York City, New Jersey, Florida or Montreal. Many still believe the Adirondack Park is run similarly to national parks and historic sites, where gates do open and close at designated times. "When do they turn the lights off?" We got that one, too.

What we have in New York state is unique. Some have called it a grand experiment. I, and about 135,000 year-round residents, like to call it home.

At almost 6 million acres in size, the Adirondack Park is about the size of Vermont. It is a patchwork of public and private lands surrounded by an imaginary Blue Line, a political boundary that gives state officials the right to regulate land within the park differently than elsewhere in the state. It's more protective inside the Blue Line. Simply put, the state Department of Environmental Conservation (DEC) manages state land, and the state Adirondack Park Agency regulates private land. Management and regulation are dictated by the ideals of conservation — protecting the natural resources of the Adirondack Park.

We do have forest rangers in the Adirondacks, but they're not taking money from tourists at the gates. There are no gates. Rangers are at trailheads and in the backcountry of the state Forest Preserve lands, helping the DEC conserve and protect the natural resources and environment of the Adirondack Mountains.

Among their many duties, they conduct searches and rescues, fight forest fires, and teach backcountry users about safely using the woods and waters.

"For Forest Rangers, public service has always offered the greatest of challenges, as it does to all men and women who can bring to it a sense of honor and dedication," wrote Louis C. Curth in his book, "The Forest Rangers: A History of the New York State Forest Ranger Force," published in 1987.

"The long heritage of devoted service found among Rangers would indicate that their stewardship for the future will be no less dedicated."

In 1985, the DEC Forest Rangers shared a centennial celebration with the New York State Forest Preserve. On May 15, 1885, Gov. David B. Hill signed legislation creating the state-owned Forest Preserve and a three-member Forest Commission to oversee the land.

Forest Preserve centennial pocket knife
Photo courtesy of the Adirondack Museum

A forest warden and forest inspectors were also hired under the law. Their top priorities were to protect the land from fire and timber theft, according to Curth.

Section 8 of the 1885 law states that the land, 681,374 acres in the Adirondacks and 33,893 acres in the Catskills, "now or hereafter constituting the Forest Preserve shall be forever kept as wild forest lands." In 1892, the New York Legislature formed the Adirondack Park, and in 1894, it adopted the "Forever Wild" clause in its constitution.

New York State Forest Ranger Limited Edition pocket knives were issued in 1985 to help celebrate the centennial, and retired Forest Ranger Peter Fish, of the Essex County town of Keene, bought one but never grew fond of it, preferring to use other knives instead. He donated the knife to the Adirondack Museum in 2000, and it is kept with a black leather sheath in a golden cardboard box. In 2003, Fish donated about 50 more items to the museum, including a green work shirt, a green wool clip-on tie, a silver Smokey Bear tie tack and his green plastic name badge.

Fish began working as a DEC forest ranger in the Catskills in 1969, calling New Paltz home. In 1975, he transferred to the Adirondacks as a forest ranger, retiring in 1998. Today he lives in the town of Keene and is still passionate about conserving the Adirondack Forest Preserve.

(This story was first published in Andy Flynn's book, "New York State's Mountain Heritage: Adirondack Attic, Volume 2.")

Adirondack Park History

ANDY FLYNN

These are ancient mountains. The Adirondack Dome — a circular dome 160 miles wide and 1 mile deep — is separate from the Appalachian mountain chain to the south and east. The Adirondack Mountains are part of the Canadian Shield with rocks more than 1 billion years old. Once much higher in elevation, they've been sculpted over time by erosion and glaciers.

Native Americans first roamed this land, using the Adirondack region as hunting grounds. Tribes from the Iroquois Confederacy — particularly the Mohawks — claimed the territory, but it was also used as hunting grounds by the Algonquins from the north and Abanakis from the east.

In 1609, French explorer Samuel de Champlain was traveling with Algonquins on Lake Champlain when they came across a band of Iroquois. The battle that ensued sparked more than 170 years of colonial strife, with the Iroquois mainly siding with the English and Algonquins siding with the French.

Beaver trapping was the first resource exploited in the Adirondacks. The Dutch claimed this region as part of New Netherland, establishing the trading post Fort Nassau (near today's Albany) on the Hudson River in 1614. The British captured the colony in 1664 and renamed it New York.

The French had claimed most of the Adirondack region as part of New France, while the British claimed it as part of New York. France and its Native American allies unsuccessfully fought Great Britain during the French and Indian War (1754-1763) for control of this land, with key battles in the region at places like Crown Point and Ticonderoga on Lake Champlain and Fort William Henry on Lake George.

The same region would be instrumental during the American Revolution and the War of 1812 against Great Britain. Again, key battles were fought along Lake Champlain.

Settlement began in the Adirondacks, mainly along the periphery, after the Revolution. The deep wilderness began to be explored and exploited for its lumber and mineral deposits (iron ore, etc.) in the early 1800s, with the first logging river drive recorded in 1813 on the Schroon River.

With millions of acres of land stripped of its wood, an environmental movement to protect the Adirondack Park began in earnest in the 1870s and reached a landmark decision in 1885 when the Adirondack Forest Preserve was established. In 1892, the Adirondack Park was created. And in 1894, the "Forever Wild" clause to the state constitution was approved, giving more stringent protection for state-owned land within the Adirondack border, known as the "Blue Line." This legislation set the stage for a strong and passionate environmental movement that continues to this day. That movement of protection was responsible for the creation of the Adirondack Park Agency in 1971.

The Adirondack Park is within a day's drive of 84 million people, including about 18 million Canadians. The pressures of development are getting greater every year. Look at the Adirondack Park from space, and you'll see how the Adirondack Park stands out. At night, the Park is dark, surrounded by the lights of cities in the U.S. and Canada. During the day, it is a sea of green, contrasted by the gray shades of development along its borders.

There are about 135,000 residents living within the Adirondack Park. With little industry here, we rely on tourism and government for most of our jobs. We call it a peopled park, one that is unique in the world, and we are continually trying to find a balance between preservation and prosperity. Can we live here and protect the park at the same time? The answer to that question will eventually determine whether the great Adirondack experiment fails or succeeds.

Log jam on an Adirondack River during a spring log drive
Photo courtesy of the Adirondack Museum

New York State DEC

DEC STAFF

The New York State Department of Environmental Conservation (DEC) was created on July 1, 1970 to combine in a single agency all state programs designed to protect and enhance the environment.

Mission: "To conserve, improve and protect New York's natural resources and environment and to prevent, abate and control water, land and air pollution in order to enhance the health, safety and welfare of the people of the state and their overall economic and social well-being."

DEC's goal is to achieve this mission through the simultaneous pursuit of environmental quality, public health, economic prosperity and social well-being, including environmental justice and the empowerment of individuals to participate in environmental decisions that affect their lives.

DEC is headed by a commissioner, who is assisted by executive managers. The department has 24 divisions and offices and is further organized into bureaus to fulfill the functions and regulations established by Title 6 of New York Codes, Rules and Regulations (6NYCRR). Some programs are also governed by federal law.

DEC's Central Office is in Albany. Each of DEC's nine regions has an office that serves the communities within that region. A total of approximately 3,000 DEC staff work in either the Central Office and the regional offices.

DEC in the Adirondack Park

All of DEC's major pollution control and natural resource programs are provided through regional staff in the Park.

New York State Environmental Conservation Law assigns DEC "care, custody and control" of the Adirondack Forest Preserve — the approximately 2.5 million acres of state-owned lands. DEC also has oversight of conservation easements on more than 750,000 acres of privately owned forest lands.

DEC forest rangers are responsible for search and rescue, wild land fire suppression and enforcing state land use laws and regulations. DEC environmental conservation officers are responsible for enforcing hunting, fishing, trapping and pollution laws and regulation.

DEC operates 42 campgrounds, five day-use areas and 78 boat launches. It also maintains more than 2,000 miles of trails, 1,300 miles of roads, 800 miles of snowmobile trails and 1,000 structures and sites trailheads, parking areas, lean-tos, bridges, pit privies, primitive campsites, bridges (vehicle, snowmobile and foot), etc.

Region 5 includes three-quarters of the Adirondack Park, with its Headquarters at 1115 State Route 86 in Ray Brook and offices in Northville and Warrensburg. The phone number at Headquarters is (518) 897-1200.

Region 6 includes the remainder of the Adirondack Park, with its Headquarters at 317 Washington St. in Watertown. The phone number at Headquarters is (315) 785-2239.

Your DEC regional office is the first place to call with specific questions such as how to obtain and renew DEC permits and how to find the best places to hunt, fish and enjoy the outdoors or to report issues involving environmental problems. Contact the Central Office with general questions about DEC policies and regulations.

DEC website: www.dec.ny.gov.

See an Adirondack Park Map with the state Forest Preserve lands on the DEC website at http://www.dec.ny.gov/docs/lands_forests_pdf/adkmap.pdf.

The DEC Region 5 Headquarters in Ray Brook informs drivers of fire danger levels.
Photo by Andy Flynn

Adirondack Park Agency

APA STAFF

The Adirondack Park Agency (APA) was created in 1971 by the New York State Legislature to develop long-range land use plans for both public and private lands within the boundary of the Park. The APA is a New York state governmental agency with an 11-member board and a staff consisting of about 60 people. The Agency Board meets monthly to act on Park policy issues and permit applications. Agency Board meetings take place the second Thursday and Friday of each month and are open to the public. Address: P.O. Box 99, 1133 State Route 86, Ray Brook, NY 12977. Phone: (518) 891-4050. Web: www.apa.ny.gov.

Responsibilities

The APA is responsible for maintaining the protection of the Forest Preserve, and overseeing development proposals of the privately owned lands. The Agency prepared the State Land Master Plan, which was signed into law in 1972, followed by the Adirondack Park Land Use and Development Plan in 1973. Both plans are periodically revised to reflect the changes and current trends and conditions of the Park. The mission of the APA is to protect the public and private resources of the Park through the exercise of the powers and duties provided by law. This mission is rooted in three statutes administered by the Agency:

1. The Adirondack Park Agency Act;
2. The New York State Freshwater Wetlands Act; and
3. The New York State Wild, Scenic, and Recreational Rivers System Act.

Advice & Service

The Agency provides several types of service to landowners considering new land use and development within the Park. These include:

•**Jurisdictional advice:** The Agency will provide a letter informing a landowner whether a permit is needed for a new land use and development or subdivision, or whether a variance is needed from the shoreline standards of the Agency. In many cases the letter advises that no permit or variance is needed. This determination is often helpful in completing financing and other arrangements related to new development in the Park.

•**Wetland advice:** The Agency will determine the location of regulated wetlands on a property or the need for a wetland permit.

•**Pre-application meeting:** A landowner proposing new land use or development can contact the Agency to schedule a pre application meeting to seek advice from agency staff on how to prepare permit applications and design projects that meet Agency regulations and guidelines.

•**Changes to the Park Plan map:** Agency staff will advise on criteria, boundaries, and the process for amendment of the official map.

•**Local Government:** Staff assists towns in the Park with the development of local planning and zoning laws as well as administering Agency-approved local land use programs.

•**Soil Science:** Staff members provide interpretations of Deep Hole Tests Pits to assist property owners in correctly locating On Site Wastewater Treatment Systems. Staff review is an extremely valuable public health service for Adirondack Park landowners.

APA Board members & designees

The Agency Board consists of eight members appointed by the governor and confirmed by the Senate, three living outside the Adirondack Park and five living inside. The other three members are the Secretary of State, Commissioner of Environmental Conservation and Commissioner of the Department of Economic Development, who send representatives to attend meetings. The Agency Board acts on Park policy issues and permit applications during Agency meetings, which are held monthly and open to the public.

Land Use and Development Plan

APA STAFF

The Adirondack Park Land Use and Development Plan applies to private land use and development in the park. The plan defines Agency jurisdiction and is designed to conserve the Park's natural resources and open-space character by directing and clustering development to minimize impact. Through the plan, all private lands are mapped into six land use classifications: Hamlet, Moderate Intensity Use, Low Intensity Use, Rural Use, Resource Management and Industrial Use. The Agency has limited jurisdiction in Hamlet areas, extensive jurisdiction in Resource Management areas, and various degrees of jurisdiction within the classification of a particular area depends on such factors as:

- existing land use and population growth patterns;
- physical limitations related to soils, slopes and elevations;
- unique features such as gorges and waterfalls;
- biological considerations; and
- public considerations.

Private Land Classification Definitions

The following are the land use area classifications of the Adirondack Park Land Use and Development Plan and a general description of their purpose:

•**Hamlet:** These are the growth and service centers of the Park where the Agency encourages development. Intentionally, the Agency has very limited permit requirements in hamlet areas. Activities there requiring an Agency permit are erecting buildings or structures over 40 feet in height, projects involving more than 100 lots, sites or units, projects involving wetlands, airports, watershed management projects, and certain expansions of buildings and uses. Hamlet boundaries usually go well beyond established settlements to provide room for future expansion.

•**Moderate Intensity Use:** Most uses are permitted; relatively concentrated residential development is most appropriate.

•**Low Intensity Use:** Most uses are permitted; residential development at a lower intensity than hamlet or moderate intensity is appropriate.

•**Rural Use:** Most uses are permitted; residential uses and reduced intensity development that preserves rural character is most suitable.

•**Resource Management:** Most development activities in resource management areas will require an Agency permit; compatible uses include residential uses, agriculture, and forestry. Special care is taken to protect the natural open space character of these lands.

•**Industrial Use:** This is where industrial uses exist or have existed, and areas which may be suitable for future industrial development. Industrial and commercial uses are also allowed in other land use area classifications.

Overall Intensity Guidelines

APA land classifications are designated to channel development into areas where it is best supported and to control the overall density of development. While very few types of activities are prohibited by the Act, some activities are prohibited in certain land use areas.

By setting limits on the amount of building — and accompanying roads, clearing, support services, etc. — the Act contemplates that the Park will retain its natural, open space character while communities in the Park continue to grow in an environmentally sensitive manner. Overall intensity guidelines are established by land use classification. While the intensity guidelines prescribe average lot sizes for building, they are not minimum lot sizes; different minimum lot sizes are also established by the Act. Only the lands owned by the project sponsor are considered when applying intensity guidelines. Existing or proposed buildings on neighbors' land do not count. See the APA map at www.apa.ny.gov.

Visitor Information

Clinton County: Information is available through the Plattsburgh-North Country Chamber of Commerce/Adirondack Coast Visitors & Convention Bureau, (877) 242-6752. Web: http://goadirondack.com.

Essex County: Information is available at the Regional Office of Sustainable Tourism (ROOST) and the Lake Placid Convention and Visitors Bureau, (800) 447-5224, with offices in Lake Placid and Crown Point. Web: www.lakeplacid.com. Additional information is provided by the Whiteface Business and Tourism Center, (888) 944-8332, www.whitefaceregion.com; the Town of Newcomb, (518) 582-3211, www.newcombny.com; the Schroon Lake Chamber of Commerce, (518)-532-7675, www.schroonlake.org; and the Ticonderoga Area Chamber of Commerce, (518) 585-6619, www.ticonderogany.com.

Franklin County: Franklin County Tourism, based in Malone, (800) 709-4895, serves communities throughout the county. Web: www.adirondacklakes.com. For more local information, try the Saranac Lake Area Chamber of Commerce, (518) 891-1990, www.saranaclake.com; or the Tupper Lake Chamber of Commerce, (518) 359-3328, www.tupper-lake.com.

Fulton County: Information is available from the Fulton County Regional Chamber of Commerce and Industry, based in Gloversville, (800) 676-3858. Web: www.44lakes.com. Additional information provided by the Northville Civic Association, (518) 863-7199, www.northvilleny.com.

Hamilton County: A wide variety of information is available from Hamilton County Tourism, Lake Pleasant, (800) 648-5239. Web: www.adirondackexperience.com. Additional information is provided by the Town of Long Lake Tourism Department, (518) 624-3077, www.longlake-ny.com; the Indian Lake Chamber of Commerce, (800) 328-5253, www.indian-lake.com; the Inlet Information Office, (315) 357-5501, www.inletny.com; and the Adirondacks Speculator Region Chamber of Commerce, (518) 548-4521. Web: www.adrkmts.com.

Farmers' market in Keene, Essex County

Photo by Andy Flynn

Main lodge at Great Camp Sagamore, Raquette Lake, Hamilton County

Photo by Andy Flynn

Lac du Saint Sacrement, a vessel from the Lake George Steamboat Company
Photo by Andy Flynn

Herkimer County: Information about the Old Forge region is available from the Town of Webb Visitor Information Center, based in Old Forge, (315) 369-6983. Web: www.old-forgeny.com.

Lewis County: Information is available from the Lewis County Chamber of Commerce, based in Lowville, (315) 376-2213. Web: www.lewiscountychamber.org.

St. Lawrence County: Information is available from the St. Lawrence County Chamber of Commerce, based in Canton, (315) 386-4000. Web: www.northcountryguide.com.

Saratoga County: Information is provided by the Saratoga Convention & Tourism Bureau, based in Saratoga Springs, (518) 584-1531. Web: www.discoversaratoga.org. Additional information is provided by the Lake Luzerne Chamber of Commerce, (518) 696-3500, www.lakeluzernechamber.org.

Warren County: The Warren County Tourism Department, based in Queensbury, (800) 958-4748, serves the entire county, including Lake George. Web: www.visitlakegeorge.com. Additional information is provided by the Lake George Regional Chamber of Commerce, (800) 705-0059, www.lakegeorgechamber.com; the Bolton Landing Chamber of Commerce, (518) 644-3831, www.boltonchamber.com; the Hague on the Lake Chamber of Commerce, (518) 543-6239, www.visithague.com; the North Warren Chamber of Commerce, based in Chestertown, (518) 494-2722, www.northwarren.com; and the Gore Mountain Region Chamber of Commerce, based in North Creek, (518) 251-2612, www.gorechamber.com.

Washington County: Information is available from Washington County Tourism, based in Fort Edward, (888) 203-8622. Web: www.washingtonnycounty.com.

The John Brown Farm State Historic Site in Lake Placid interprets the history of this famous abolitionist's life, especially his brief time in the Adirondack Park. The site includes Brown's grave.

Photo by Andy Flynn

Take a seaplane ride with Helms Aero Service in Long Lake, Hamilton County.

Photo by Andy Flynn

Blue Mt. House Chamber Pot

ANDY FLYNN

Let's mention one of the unmentionables for a moment, and, since we're mostly grownups here, I can hopefully mention the chamber pot without anyone giggling or gasping or writing a letter to the editor. The truth is, human waste disposal is a simple fact of life, and it is as much a part of our hospitality history in the Adirondacks as the bed or the bill. Just ask Lake Placid village officials as they ponder another Olympic bid.

For the most part, Americans today are spoiled by indoor plumbing, and they leave the historical question of "Where did they do that back then?" to the imagination because very few history books will indulge their curiosity of where patrons "did that" in hotels prior to flush toilets. Sure, we take photographs of outhouses and romanticize their use on cute posters and in slick coffee table books, but don't ask most Americans to use one, with spiders in the dark corners, splintered seats gnawed on by porcupines, and that dark, stinky hole. What's down there? Is it safe to…well, you know…sit on it and…use it?

Get over it. If you gotta go, you gotta go. That is most apparent to backpackers tramping through the deepest wilderness areas of the Adirondacks, where they may not even have the luxury of using a brown-stained outhouse that offers privacy from spying eyes and protection from mosquitoes and blackflies. ("How did you get a bite down there?") They simply dig a cat hole and do their thing.

I imagine all the old Adirondack hotels had outhouses for the owners, workers and patrons, although I don't see too many of these bathroom structures in historical photographs of the hotels. Water closets were not in general use until the mid 1880s in the United States, even later in remote parts of the country such as the Adirondack Mountains. People were left with chamber pots and commodes for in-room relief.

The six-story, 300-room Prospect House in Blue Mountain Lake, a hotel opening in 1882, was a state-of-the-art facility at the time. It was the first hotel in the world to have Edison electric lights in every bedroom. Each room had running water, and the bathhouse at the rear of the hotel featured hot and cold running water, according to Harold Hochschild in "An

The log hotel at the Adirondack Museum was part of the Blue Mountain House.

Photo by Andy Flynn

Chamber pot used at the Blue Mountain House in Blue Mountain Lake

Photo courtesy of the Adirondack Museum

Adirondack Resort in the Nineteenth Century, Blue Mountain Lake, 1870-1900, Stage-coaches and Luxury Hotels." He tells the story of the hotel's unique outhouse:

"Adjoining the bathhouse was one of the hotel's most spectacular innovations, an elaborately constructed outhouse of not one but two stories, each connected with the hotel, so that guests would not have to brave the elements and those from the upper floors would not have to descend all the way to the main floor. The outhouse was, of course, without benefit of plumbing, then virtually unknown for that purpose except in a few well-to-do homes."

A couple of miles away, on the western slope of Blue Mountain, lived Miles Tyler Merwin. His was not a well-to-do home, and his modest hotel, the Blue Mountain House, was not as opulent as Frederick C. Durant's Prospect House. Merwin opened his log hotel in 1874 and built another log cottage in 1876. At the time, the hostelry could accommodate 40 guests. The original hotel was destroyed by fire in February 1880, and a new three-story frame structure was constructed in the spring, opening to the public in July 1880.

The 1876 log hotel, with an annex in the back, is the only structure from the Blue Mountain House still standing. It is now an exhibit building at the Adirondack Museum, which was built on Merwin's former property. Merwin sold the Blue Mountain House in 1935 to W.L. Wessels, who sold it in 1954 to the Adirondack Historical Association. The three-story structure was replaced in 1955 by the main building of the Adirondack Museum.

While preparing to open the Adirondack Museum in 1957, founder Harold Hochschild began collecting historical artifacts from the Adirondack region. He started close to home, with Merwin's former hotel, including more than 10 chamber pots used in the guest rooms. They help answer the question, "Where did they do that back then?" But they don't answer the questions, "Who cleaned the rooms?" and "Where did they empty the pots?"

Vacuuming rooms, making beds and scrubbing toilets is one of the least glamorous jobs in any hotel. I've done my share at places like the Adirondak Loj in Lake Placid. Yet, if there was a bright side to Adirondack chambermaid work in the 21st century, it would shine brightly in the orange glow of a sauna light in the bathroom, where modern plumbing and flush toilets have thankfully taken over the hands-on waste disposal task from human beings. Progress can be a good thing.

(This story was first published in Andy Flynn's book, "New York State's Mountain Heritage: Adirondack Attic, Volume 4.")

Special Event Highlights

There are too many events in the Adirondack Park throughout the year to name here: craft fairs, lecture series, carnivals, concerts, plays, sporting events, fishing derbies, art shows, agricultural festivals, townwide garage sales, quilt shows, etc. These are simply the highlights that would fit the space. For more, contact your local tourism office.

Historic AARCH Tours: Each year, Keeseville-based Adirondack Architectural Heritage (AARCH) sponsors a series of guided tours to historic places. Phone: (518) 834-9328. Web: www.aarch.org.

Living History Events at Fort Ticonderoga: The fort hosts a number of living history programs throughout the summer season, including encampments that tell the story of the historical events that unfolded here during the French & Indian War and American Revolution. Phone: (518) 585-2821. Web: www.fortticonderoga.org.

Farmers' Markets: Find fresh food and crafts at farmers' markets during the summer and fall months throughout the Adirondack region. Here is the schedule: MONDAY, 9 a.m. - 1 p.m., June-Sept., **Schroon Lake**, Town Hall parking lot; TUESDAY, 10 a.m. - 2 p.m., May-Oct., **Saranac Lake**, Fusion Market; WEDNESDAY, 9 a.m. - 1 p.m., June-Oct., **Lake Placid**, LPCA; WEDNESDAY, 9 a.m. - 1 p.m., June-Aug., **Keeseville**, Riverside Park; WEDNESDAY, 10 a.m. - 2 p.m., June-Oct., **Chestertown**, Chester Town Hall; WEDNESDAY, 9 a.m. - 1 p.m., June-Aug., **Port Henry**, Boni's Bistro parking lot, Main Street; THURSDAY, 10 a.m. - 2 p.m., June-Aug., **Long Lake**, corner of Routes 28N/30 and South Hill Road across from the post office; THURSDAY, 3-6 p.m., June-Oct., **North Creek**, Adirondack Tri-County Nursing & Rehabilitation Center; THURSDAY, 3:30-6:30 p.m., June-Sept., **Willsboro**, Route 22 south of Champlain National Bank; THURSDAY, 11 a.m. - 3 p.m., June-Sept., The Wild Center, **Tupper Lake**; FRIDAY, 9 a.m. - 1 p.m., June-Aug., **Bolton Landing**, Blessed Sacrament Church parking lot; FRIDAY, 3-6 p.m., May-Oct., **Warrensburg**, Warrensburgh Riverfront, River Street near Curtis Lumber; FRIDAY, 3-6 p.m., June-Aug., **Au Sable Forks**, Riverside Park; FRIDAY, 9 a.m. - 1 p.m., May-Oct., **Elizabethtown**, Adirondack Center Museum; FRIDAY, 2-5 p.m., June-Sept., **Paul Smiths**, Paul Smith's College VIC; FRIDAY, 10 a.m. - 4 p.m., June-Sept., **Diamond Point**, Community Church; SATURDAY, 9 a.m. - 2 p.m., June-Oct., **Saranac Lake**, Riverside Park; SATURDAY, 10 a.m. - 1 p.m., June-Oct., **Ticonderoga**, corner of Montcalm and 9N, SW of Moses Circle; SATURDAY, 9 a.m. - 2 p.m., July-Sept., **Indian Lake**, Indian Lake Central School; SATURDAY, 10 a.m. - 2 p.m., June-Aug., **Chateaugay Lakes**, SR 374, Lawn of the Hollywood Inn; and SUNDAY, 9:30 a.m. - 2 p.m., June-Oct., **Keene**, Marcy Airfield. Learn more online at the **Adirondack Harvest** website at www.adirondackharvest.com. (These times were from 2013 and may change.)

JANUARY: The **Adirondack Ice Bowl** is an annual two-day pond-hockey tournament held on Fourth Lake in the Hamilton County town of Inlet. Web: http://inletny.com.

FEBRUARY: The 10-day **Saranac Lake Winter Carnival** dates to 1897 and features a Coronation Ceremony, Lighting of the Ice Palace, sporting events, fireworks, concerts, a Gala Parade and more. Web: www.saranaclakewintercarnival.com.

FEBRUARY: The **Lake George Winter Carnival** is a month-long celebration that features events on weekends in February. Web: www.lakegeorgewintercarnival.com.

FEBRUARY: Feb Fest in Speculator is a month-long celebration and includes the Winter Carnival at Oak Mountain Ski Center. Web: http://speculatorchamber.com.

FEBRUARY: The **Empire State Winter Games** are held in Lake Placid and Wilmington and feature young athletes competing in winter sports such as alpine skiing, bobsled, cross-country skiing, figure skating, ice hockey, luge, skeleton, snowshoe racing, speed

Concert in Bolton Landing, Warren County

Photo by Andy Flynn

skating and ski jumping. Web: www.empirestatewintergames.com.

MARCH: Snofest is held in Old Forge and marks the end of the snowmobiling season in this part of the Adirondacks. Phone: (315) 369-6983. Web: www.SnoFestNY.com.

MARCH: Join maple producers for a month-long festival at the **Thurman Maple Days**, highlighted by a Jackwax Party (sugar on snow). Web: www.thurmanmapledays.com.

MARCH: During the two-week celebration called **Maple Weekend**, maple syrup producers throughout the state, including the Adirondack Park, open their sugar shacks and demonstrate how they make the state's sweetest product. Web: www.mapleweekend.com.

APRIL/MAY: Daffest in Saranac Lake features the region's biggest soapboax derby and various events while celebrating the arrival of daffodils. Web: www.daffest.com.

MAY: The annual **Hudson River White Water Derby** is held in North River and North Creek and features racing with kayaks and canoes. Web: http://whitewaterderby.com.

JUNE: The annual **Adirondack Boreal Birding Festival** in Hamilton County highlights the boreal bird species of the Adirondack Park with lectures, hikes, canoe trips, walks and seminars. Web: www.adirondackbirds.com.

JUNE: The annual **Americade** motorbike event is held in Lake George and includes tours throughout the region. It is dubbed the world's largest touring rally. Phone: (518) 798-7888. Web: http://americade.com.

JUNE: The **Lake Placid Film Forum** features movies, forums and classes. Web: www.lakeplacidfilmforum.com.

JUNE/JULY: The **Lake Placid Horse Show** and the **I Love New York Horse Show** are held for two weeks at the North Elba Horse Show Grounds, Lake Placid and feature world-class competition. Phone: (518) 523-9625. Web: www.lakeplacidhorseshow.com.

JULY: The **Tupper Lake Woodsmen's Days** are held the second weekend in July. The event celebrates the community's logging heritage. Phone: (518) 359-9444. Web: www.woodsmendays.com.

JULY: The **Adirondack Storytelling Festival** is at McCauley Mountain Ski Area, Old Forge. It is co-sponsored by the Old Forge Library. Phone: (315) 369-6008.

JULY: The annual **Rondeaufest** music festival is held at the Mount Sabattis pavilion in Long Lake. Phone: (518) 624-3077. Web: www.longlake-ny.com.

JULY: Ironman USA Lake Placid returns to the Olympic region in late July every year. Held on a Sunday with a start at Mirror Lake and finish at the Speed Skating Oval, it includes a 2.4-mile swim, 116-mile bike race and 26.2-mile run. Web: www.ironmanusa.com.

JULY/AUGUST: The **Essex County Fair** is held at the fairgrounds in Westport. Enjoy live music, food, demolition derby, 4-H demonstrations, horse shows, tractor/truck pulls, harness racing, and the Roll Over Contest. Web: www.essexcountyfair.org.

AUGUST: The annual **Can-Am Rugby Tournament** is one of the largest and best run tournaments of its kind in the world and includes competition of more than 100 teams in Saranac Lake and Lake Placid. Web: http://canamrugby.com.

AUGUST: The annual **Durant Days** is held in early August at Raquette Lake and includes tours of Great Camps, kids' activities and fireworks. Web: www.longlake-ny.com.

AUGUST: The **Adirondack Folk Music Festival** is at the Schroon Lake Town Park. Phone: (518) 532-9259. Web: www.schroonlakearts.com.

AUGUST: Adirondack Authors Night is held the second Tuesday of August from 7 to 9 p.m. at Hoss's Country Corner, Long Lake. Phone: (800) 952-4677. Web: www.hosss-countrycorner.com.

AUGUST: The **Adirondack Museum Antiques Show** is held in Blue Mountain Lake. Phone: (518) 352-7311. Web: www.adkmuseum.org.

AUGUST: The annual **Upper Hudson Bluegrass Festival** is held at the Ski Bowl Park in North Creek. Web: http://upperhudsonbluegrassfestival.com.

SEPTEMBER: Teddy Roosevelt Weekend in Newcomb celebrates the community's historic link to the 26th U.S. president, Theodore Roosevelt. Web: www.newcombny.com.

SEPTEMBER: The **Rustic Furniture Fair** is held at the Adirondack Museum in Blue Mountain Lake. Phone: (518) 352-7311. Web: www.adkmuseum.org.

SEPTEMBER: The town of Inlet's annual **Fall Festival** is held at Fern Park and features entertainment, vendors, food and much more. Web: www.inletny.com.

SEPTEMBER: The annual **Oktoberfest** is held at the Whiteface Mountain Ski Center in Wilmington. Web: www.whitefacelakeplacid.com.

SEPTEMBER: The **Great Adirondack Moose Festival** is held in Indian Lake. Web: www.indian-lake.com.

SEPTEMBER/OCTOBER: The **World's Largest Garage Sale** features hundreds of vendors in the town of Warrensburg for a weekend full of treasure hunting. Sponsored by the Warrensburg Chamber of Commerce. Web: www.warrensburgchamber.com.

OCTOBER: The annual **Harvest Fest** is held at the Gore Mountain Ski Center in North Creek. Web: www.goremountain.com.

DECEMBER: Snodeo is held in Old Forge and marks the start of the snowmobiling season in this part of the Adirondacks. Phone: (315) 369-6983.

Staying Safe in Moose Country

Moose are much larger and taller than deer. The large body causes greater damage, and, when struck, the height often causes them to impact the windshield of a car or pickup truck, not just the front of the vehicle.

Early Fall is the breeding season for moose in northern New York. During this time moose are wandering looking for mates, leading them to areas where they are not typically seen. While this improves the opportunities for people to enjoy sighting of a moose, it also increases the danger of colliding with one on the roadway. Moose are most active at dawn and dusk, which are times of poor visibility. Moose are especially difficult to see at night because of their dark brown to black coloring and their height — which puts their head and much of their body above vehicle headlights.

Take the following precautions to prevent moose vehicle collisions:

• Use extreme caution when driving at dawn or dusk, especially during September and October.

• Reduce your speed, stay alert and watch the roadsides.

• Slow down when approaching moose standing near the roadside, as they may bolt at the last minute when a car comes closer.

• Moose may travel in pairs or small groups, so if a moose is spotted crossing the road, be alert for others that may follow.

• Make sure all vehicle occupants wear seat belts and children are properly restrained in child safety seats.

• Use flashers or a headlight signal to warn other drivers when moose are spotted near the road.

• Motorcyclists should be especially alert for moose.

• If a moose runs in front of your vehicle, brake firmly but do not swerve. Swerving can cause a vehicle-vehicle collision or cause the vehicle to hit a fixed object such as a tree or pole.

• If a moose is hit and killed by a vehicle, the motorist should not remove the animal unless a permit is obtained from the investigating officer at the scene.

Our Olympic Heritage

ANDY FLYNN

Adirondack residents are proud of their Olympic heritage, not just because we have hosted two Olympic Winter Games (in 1932 and 1980) in Lake Placid but because this village and surrounding towns consistently send young athletes to the Olympics every four years. The Olympic venues, operated by the New York **Olympic Regional Development Authority (ORDA)**, give local athletes a chance to train on their home turf.

Above all, for local athletes who live in or near Lake Placid, there is one beacon of hope that keeps them focused on their Olympic dreams: The 1980 Olympic cauldron, which still stands at the North Elba Horse Show Grounds. It is a reminder of our Olympic roots, dating to 1924 when Lake Placid resident Charles Jewtraw won the first winter gold medal — for speed skating — during the first Olympic Winter Games in Chamonix.

In 1981, legislation established ORDA, which assumed management, operation and promotion of the Olympic facilities in October 1982 as a result of a state constitutional amendment. ORDA manages the **Olympic Sports Complex** at Mount Van Hoevenberg (site of the 1932 and 1980 Olympic Winter Games bobsled races and the 1980 luge, cross-country and biathlon competition), the 1932 and 1980 **Olympic arenas** (home of the "Miracle on Ice" hockey game between the USSR and USA in 1980), the **Lake Placid Winter Olympic Museum**, the Speed Skating Oval (site of 1932 and 1980 competition), **Ski Jumping Complex** (site of 1932 and 1980 competition), and the **Whiteface Mountain** (site of 1980 alpine competition) and **Gore Mountain** ski areas in the Adirondacks and **Belleayre Mountain** ski center in the Catskills. Phone: (518) 523-1655. Web: www.whitefacelakeplacid.com.

Located at the corner of Old Military Road and Church Street, the **United States Olympic Training Center** consists of a main support building, two housing unit clusters, a field house with indoor surfaces and weight rooms, and groomed outdoor fields. The facility houses almost 300 athletes in hotel-style rooms. Web: www.teamusa.org.

USA Luge, based in Lake Placid, is the National Governing Body for the sport of luge in the U.S. and was formed in 1979. The York International Luge Training Complex, located here, is one of only two start ramp facilities in North America. Open-year round, the facility contains three fully enclosed, refrigerated and elevated start-training ramps that enable athletes to practice their start technique. Phone: (518) 523-2071. Web: www.usaluge.org.

Here is the Olympic speed skating oval and Olympic Center arena on Main Street, Lake Placid. On the outside rink, speed skater Eric Heiden won five gold medals during the 1980 Olympic Winter Games. On the inside rink is the home of the "Miracle on Ice," where the men's ice hockey team won the game against the Soviet Union in 1980.

Photo by Andy Flynn

Olympic Ski Jumping Complex, Lake Placid, Essex County

Photo by Andy Flynn

1930s Bobsled Mask

ANDY FLYNN

This is the story about two Olympic Winter Games, one in the U.S. and one in Germany, and a New York City man who found his need for speed on a bobsled run.

John "Donna" Fox, a mortician from Tremont, N.Y. in the Bronx, was 35 years old when he first visited Lake Placid during the 1932 Olympic Winter Games. It was a vacation that would change his life forever. He fell in love with the Adirondack Mountains and a sport that was new to him: bobsledding.

As a child, Fox yearned to race cars, but his parents wouldn't let him. Driving a bobsled was his chance to finally get adrenaline rushing through his system, and after his first ride, he was hooked. Little did the world know it would take just a few years for Lake Placid to turn this Bronxite into an Olympic athlete.

From the many newspaper clippings in his scrapbook, it is apparent that Fox enjoyed competition, a good adrenaline rush and making headlines. Ironically, he chose a more docile sport to challenge himself and others during the summer: golf. Fox seemed to excel at whatever he put his mind to, and golf and bobsledding gave him a year-round schedule to fill his competitive needs in the 1930s.

The Adirondack Museum now owns a leather helmet/mask Fox used in the 1930s while bobsledding in Lake Placid.

The outside of the leather helmet is painted red, white and blue, and the inside is lined with fleece. It features a solid skull cap and a face mask with large eye, nose and ear holes and many small, circular vents. It measures 10.5 inches tall and 23 inches in circumference.

There is mystery attached to this unique helmet. At the forehead of the skull cap, in a circle, is a maker's mark: "A.G. Spaulding & Bros." Yet, notes in the museum's accession file state that the helmet was designed by Fox for the 1935 Olympic tryout races in Lake Placid. Look closely. Take away the mask, and you have a helmet identical to the ones bobsledders were using in the early 1930s, complete with the skull cap and ear protection. Since it gets frigid on the bobsled run, perhaps Fox took an existing helmet and had a blue-painted leather mask attached to it. Since he spent countless hours constructing and fine-tuning his bobsleds during the off-season, it makes sense that he would pay special attention to his headgear.

Adding to the mystery, there is a set of initials scratched into the back of the helmet, and they aren't "J.F." or "D.F." They are "P.S." Perhaps Fox acquired the helmet from another bobsledder before adding the mask and using it to win the four-man bobsled race during the 1935 American Olympic tryouts. Could this person be Paul Stevens? It's possible.

The heroes of the 1932 Olympic two-man bobsled team, USA 1, were J. Hubert and Curtis Stevens, of Lake Placid, who earned a gold medal. Their brother, F. Paul Stevens, took home a silver medal as part of the USA 2 four-man bobsled team. It wasn't long before Fox introduced himself to the Stevens brothers and took his first ride down the Mount Van Hoevenberg bobsled run in a two-man sled with Curtis.

After a few practice runs, he joined the half-mile novice event and was fully committed to racing bobsleds in amateur events during the winter of 1932-33.

In a 1933 newspaper story with the headline, "Bronx mortician defies icy death," Fox described his love for the sport:

"Flying down the run with the speed of the wind gives me a thrill which can't be found any where else. A man has to be in good physical shape to compete. It's a real exercise to steer or to be an expert 'bobber.' And dangerous, too.

"On three of the curves of the Mount Van Hoevenberg run, I've been 'out,' or unconscious, for the fleeting part of a second. It's due to the air pressure. Just before I feel my-

This bobsled mask was used in the 1930s in Lake Placid.

Photo courtesy of the Adirondack Museum

self 'going,' I turn the wheel a trifle in case we hit a rut. The air pressure feels like a house on your back, but you come right out of it, or at least I have so far."

A Feb. 20, 1934 news story by Harry Cross shows just how cold it was during some of the bobsled races. Cross was covering the North American Championships for the two-man event, which was postponed because of 12-below temperatures and a snowstorm.

"Four of the drivers [including Fox] found when they reached the bottom that their faces were frozen," Cross wrote. "Snow and ice were quickly applied to relieve the situation."

During the 1935 season, Fox raced his two-man sled but actually gained a seat on the 1936 Olympic team by driving the winning four-man sled during the American tryouts in February 1935. At the same time, he broke the 1.5-mile course record.

There were 15 spots on the 1936 U.S. Olympic bobsled team, and many Adirondackers filled those positions along with Fox, including Ivan E. Brown and Allan M. Washbond, of Keene Valley; and J. Hubert Stevens and Curtis Stevens, of Lake Placid. A newspaper story, dated Dec. 27, 1935, reported that Curtis Stevens withdrew from the team "for business reasons." Only 14 U.S. bobsledders would head to the Bavarian Alps for the 1936 Olympic Winter Games in Garmisch-Partenkirchen, Germany.

A Feb. 8, 1936 trial run would cost Fox his dreams of Olympic gold. He crashed a four-man sled on the final curve "with [the] record in sight," according to a news clipping. The other three bobsledders — James Bickford, Max T. Bly and Richard W. Lawrence — escaped with scratches. Fox, however, suffered a "deep gash over the knee and a cruelly wrenched ankle." Despite Fox's pleas to compete, U.S. Olympic officials wouldn't let him. Francis Tyler, of Lake Placid, replaced him as the driver and finished sixth. It was the Keene Valley duo of Brown and Washbond that took home gold in 1936 for the two-man bobsled.

(This story was first published in Andy Flynn's book, "New York State's Mountain Heritage: Adirondack Attic, Volume 4.")

Major Attractions

The **Adirondack Carousel**, located on Depot Street in Saranac Lake, is open year-round, and hours vary depending on the season. Riders can choose from 18 moving wildlife figures that include a Large Mouthed Bass, Bobcat, Black Fly and Loon; and the all-accessible Chris-Craft style chariot. Phone: (518) 891-9521. Web: www.adirondackcarousel.org.

The **Adirondack Folk School**, located at 51 Main St. in Lake Luzerne, is the only school of its kind in the country dedicated to teaching the arts, crafts and culture of this unique Adirondack region. Subjects at this non-profit school include Adirondack chair building, twig and rustic furniture, caning, paddle making, birch bark basketry, fly tying, weaving, organic gardening, fiber arts, soap making, pottery and blacksmithing. Phone: (518) 696-2400. Web: www.adirondackfolkschool.org.

The **Adirondack History Center Museum** is located on Hand Avenue in Elizabethtown. It is home to the Essex County Historical Society and displays artifacts from over two centuries of life in Essex County. Phone: (518) 873-6466. Web: www.adkhistorycenter.org.

The **Adirondack Lakes Center for the Arts**, located on Route 28N in the hamlet of Blue Mountain Lake, is a big city arts center in the middle of the wilderness, offering a variety of arts activities for residents and visitors: concerts, art and photography exhibits, plays, workshops, classes, special events and the Arts Center Pre-School (ages 2 1/2 to 5). Phone: (518) 352-7715. Web: http://adirondackarts.org.

The **Adirondack Museum**, located on Route 28N/30 in Blue Mountain Lake, tells the story of the Adirondacks through exhibits, special events and classes for schools and hands-on activities for visitors of all ages. It is open daily from Memorial Day weekend to mid-October. Phone: (518) 352-7311. Web: www.adkmuseum.org.

The **Adirondack Scenic Railroad** offers scenic train rides from the historic Thendara, Saranac Lake and Lake Placid train stations in the summer. Phone: (800) 819-2291. Web: www.adirondackrr.com.

Step back in time at **Ausable Chasm** as you follow the trails of the oldest natural attraction in the United States. Adventures include tubing, lantern tours, cave and waterfall hikes, river ducky trip, mountain bike tour, horseback riding and winter tours. Phone: (518) 834-7454. Web: www.ausablechasm.com.

The **Adirondack Interpretive Center**, located on State Route 28N in Newcomb, is operated by the SUNY College of Environmental Science & Forestry's Adirondack Ecological Center. It offers programs, special events and a trail system (used for hiking, snowshoeing and cross-country skiing). Open year-round. Phone: (518) 582-2000. Web: http://www.esf.edu/aic.

The **Barton Mines Garnet Tours** are available during the summer and early fall. Located on the Barton Mines Road in North River, visitors will learn about the world's largest garnet deposit here in the Adirondacks on Gore Mountain and search for their own garnet. Phone: (518) 251-2706. Web: www.garnetminetours.com.

The **Crown Point State Historic Site**, operated by New York state, interprets Fort St. Frederic, built by the French in the 1730s, and His Majesty's Fort at Crown Point, built by the British from 1759 to 1763. Both were used during the French and Indian War. It is open in the summer. Phone: (518) 597-4666. Web: www.nysparks.state.ny.us.

The **Depot Theatre** offers repertory theater in the summer at the historic 1876 train station on Main Street in Westport. Phone: (518) 962-8680. Web: http://depottheatre.org.

The **Enchanted Forest/Water Safari**, Old Forge, offers rides and attractions for families and is the only water park in the Adirondacks. Phone: (315) 369-6145. Web: www.watersafari.com.

The Wild Center, Tupper Lake, Franklin County

Photo by Andy Flynn

Ruins at the Crown Point State Historic Site, Essex County

Photo by Andy Flynn

Fort Ticonderoga, a National Historic Landmark, is a restored fort dating to 1755, when the French began building it as Fort Carillon. The British took it over in 1759 during the French and Indian War, re-naming it Fort Ticonderoga, and it was used by British and American troops during the American Revolution. It opened to the public in 1909. Phone: (518) 585-2821. Web: www.fort-ticonderoga.org.

The British-built **Fort William Henry**, in Lake George, commanded the southern end of Lake George from 1755 to 1757, during the French and Indian War. Visit this museum and restoration. Open in the summer. Phone: (518) 668-5471. Web: www.fwhmuseum.com.

Great Camp Sagamore, a National Historic Landmark in Raquette Lake, is the only Adirondack Great Camp open to the public for overnight stays. It was the wilderness estate of the Vanderbilt family from 1901 to 1954. Phone: (315) 354-5311. Web: www.greatcampsagamore.org.

High Falls Gorge: In the shadow of Whiteface Mountain, visitors can take a nature walk to view the West Branch of the Ausable River as it spills over ancient granite cliffs. Open year-round. Phone: (518) 946-2278. Web: www.highfallsgorge.com.

John Brown Farm State Historic Site: Its appearance and historic documents have been restored in tribute to this famous abolitionist who came into the Adirondacks in 1849 and who was buried here 10 years later after being hanged for treason. The farm site is open seasonally. Phone: (518) 523-3900. Web: www.nysparks.com.

The **Lake George Steamboat Company** offers summer boat tours on the Mohican, Minne-Ha-Ha, and Lac du Saint Sacrement. Phone: (518) 668-5777. Web: www.lakegeorgesteamboat.com.

The **Lake Placid Center for the Arts** has long been a hub of cultural activity in the Tri-Lakes region. The Center, located at 17 Algonquin Dr., offers a full calendar of events including live theater, concerts and film series for adults and children and provides facilities and technical assistance to many arts organizations. Performances by leading dance companies are a highlight of the summer. Gallery exhibitions and foreign films are also featured. Phone: (518) 523-2512. Web: www.lakeplacidarts.org.

Natural Stone Bridge and Caves, Pottersville, offers summer and winter tours of a massive stone bridge arch — the largest marble cave entrance in the East — raging waterfalls and tranquil dark pools. Phone: (518) 494-2283. Web: www.stonebridgeandcaves.com.

At the **Old Forge Lake Cruises**, see the Fulton Chain of Lakes from the decks of Clearwater, Zilpha or President Harrison. Your cruise will follow the old steamboat route through the lakes. Phone: (315) 369-6473. Web: www.oldforgelakecruises.com.

Olympic Venues: The Olympic Regional Development Authority (ORDA) operates the **Olympic Sports Complex** at Mount Van Hoevenberg (trails for cross-country skiing, snowshoeing, and mountain biking, plus a luge/bobsled/skeleton track), the **Whiteface Mountain Ski Center** in Wilmington, the **Gore Mountain Ski Center** in North Creek, the **Olympic Ski Jumping Complex**, the **Olympic Speed Skating Oval**, the **Lake Placid Winter Olympic Museum** and the **Olympic Center**. Phone: (518) 523-1655. Web: www.whitefacelakeplacid.com.

The **Paul Smith's College VIC**, located on State Route 30 in Paul Smiths, is a visitor interpretive center that offers programs, special events and a year-round trail system. See the Butterfly House in the summer. Open year-round. Phone: (518) 327-6241.

Pendragon Theatre, 15 Brandy Brook Ave. in Saranac Lake, is the only year-round professional theater in the Park. Phone: (518) 891-1854. Web: www.pendragontheatre.org.

Railroads on Parade, Route 9 in Pottersville, is a 5,000-square-foot building that houses five magical worlds of model trains: The Station, The Hell Gate Bridge, Park Avenue/Subways, The 1939 World's Fair and The Prince Edward Island Railway. Created by Clarke Dunham. Open in the summer. Phone: (518) 623-0100. Web: www.railroadsonparade.com.

Six Nations Indian Museum, Onchiota, Franklin County

Photo by Andy Flynn

The **Raquette Lake Navigation Company** offers dine and cruise boat tours on Raquette Lake on the W.W. Durant. Phone: (315) 354-5532. Web: www.raquettelakenavigation.com.

The **Robert Louis Stevenson Memorial Cottage & Museum**, located at 44 Stevenson Lane in Saranac Lake, is where the immortal "R.L.S." spent the winter of 1887-88 and wrote the genesis of "The Master of Ballantrae." Open July 1 to Columbus Day or by appointment. Phone: (518) 891-1462. Web: www.robertlouisstevensonmemorialcottage.org.

At the **Santa's Workshop** theme park, located at 324 Whiteface Memorial Highway in Wilmington, families can celebrate the magic of Christmas with a visit to Santa Claus at the North Pole, N.Y. Phone: (800) 806-0215. Web: www.northpoleny.com.

The **Saratoga & North Creek Railway** offers daily passenger service Memorial Day weekend to Oct. 31 plus a Snow Train in the winter from Saratoga Springs to North Creek. Phone: (877) 726-7245. Web: www.sncrr.com.

At the **Six Nations Indian Museum**, Onchiota, see 3,000-plus artifacts with an emphasis on the Six Nations of the Iroquois Confederacy and storytelling lectures. Open July 1-Labor Day. Phone: (518) 891-2299. Web: http://sixnationsindianmuseum.com.

The **Veterans' Memorial Highway** up to the Whiteface Mountain Observatory, 8 miles of scenic highway, rises toward the spectacular summit of Whiteface Mountain. Web: www.whitefacelakeplacid.com.

The **View arts center in Old Forge**, located at 3273 State Route 28, offers art exhibits, workshops, performances and special events in a 28,000-square-foot building that houses a state-of-the-art performance hall, expanded exhibition galleries and fine arts workshop studios. Phone: (315) 369-6411. Web: www.viewarts.org.

The **Wild Center** is located at 45 Museum Dr. in Tupper Lake. There are walking trails, naturalist guides, movies and live exhibits including more than 900 live animals. Phone: (518) 359-7800. Web: www.wildcenter.org.

Recreation

There are countless recreational opportunities inside the 6-million-acre Adirondack Park. If you hear someone say, "I'm bored. There's nothing to do," then they really don't appreciate what this region has to offer. With lakes and rivers at your front door, and mountains at your back door, take some time to explore this amazing oasis, a park for the people.

Hiking: Given the sturdy heart and stout boots to get him there — and a compass lest he stray from the trails — anyone may roam these acres as he chooses providing that he observes a few simple rules laid down by the New York State Department of Environmental Conservation (DEC). Even experienced woodsmen do not venture into the wilderness without taking every precaution for safety. Learn more at the DEC web site: www.dec.ny.gov. Hiking guides for all regions of the Park are published through the Adirondack Mountain Club, (518) 523-3441, www.adk.org. Check your local gift shop/bookstore.

Outfitters: There are a number of excellent businesses ready to outfit you on a paddling tour through the Adirondack Mountains.

Guides: Choose a New York state licensed guide to lead you on a memorable Adirondack adventure through the wilderness, from paddling and hiking to fishing, rock climbing and birding. Find one at the New York State Outdoor Guides Association: www.nysoga.com.

Boating: For an Adirondack Waterways guide, contact the Adirondack Regional Tourism Council at (518) 846-8016. Web: http://visitadirondacks.com.

The 740-mile **Northern Forest Canoe Trail** features some of the most scenic paddling country in the Northeast from Old Forge, N.Y. to Fort Kent, Maine. The 147-mile New York section spans from the Old Forge to Lake Champlain. Web: www.northernforestcanoe-trail.org.

Birding and Nature Hiking

The Adirondack Park contains some of the most diverse wildlife habitats in the Northeast.

One of the unique habitats of the Adirondacks is the boreal forest. Containing features such as open river corridors, conifer swamps, floating peatlands, and beaver meadows, the boreal forest contains birds at the southernmost extent of their range in eastern North America. These birds, such as rusty blackbirds, black-backed woodpeckers and boreal chickadees, are uncommon in much of the rest of the Northeast and make the Adirondacks a significant part of the region's breeding bird diversity.

More common birds, including several species of flycatchers and sparrows, can be found along roadsides near open fields. Great blue herons, ducks, and other wetland birds can be found along beaver ponds, open wetlands and shorelines along rivers. The majestic common loon can often be seen in ponds and lakes throughout the Adirondacks. Look for its stunning black and white plumage and low profile as it glides through the water. You may get a glimpse of the loon fishing or hear its signature call while traveling through the park.

Early morning is the time birds sing on their territory and attract mates. Be sure to bring a good pair of binoculars and try to remain quiet. A professional naturalist can also help you enjoy the region's wildlife. With the many miles of hiking trails that go through wildlife habitat, you are bound to see birds, fox, deer, small mammals, and maybe even a moose somewhere along your walk.

Hunting: In New York's Northern Zone, hunters take to the woods each fall with bows, muzzleloaders and rifles. Hunting is permitted on all state lands, so the hunting territory is considerable. Please be considerate of posted private lands. Regular deer and bear season is from late October to early December. Learn more at www.dec.ny.gov.

Fishing: Anglers can try to catch their fish year-round throughout the Park. The DEC stocks many of the waterways with several species. Fishing regulations are available at the DEC: www.dec.ny.gov. Learn more about fly fishing in Wilmington at www.whitefaceregion.com/recreation/fishing/hatch-schedule.

Cross-country skiing: People can share trails with snowshoers or visit one of the many golf courses or cross-country ski centers in the Park. Popular destinations include: **Lapland Lake Nordic Vacation Center** in Northville (www.laplandlake.com); **Mount Van Hoevenberg Cross-Country Ski Center** in Lake Placid (www.whiteface.com); **Dewey Mountain Recreation Center** in Saranac Lake (www.deweymountain.com); and **Garnet Hill Lodge Cross-Country Ski Center** in North River (www.garnet-hill.com). Contact your local tourism office for the nearest center.

Downhill skiing: Facilities in the Adirondack Park include: **Gore Mountain** and the **Ski Bowl**, North Creek (www.goremountain.com); **Whiteface Mountain**, Wilmington (www.whiteface.com); **McCauley Mountain**, Old Forge (http://mccauleyny.com); **Oak Mountain**, Speculator (http://oakmountainski.com); **Mount Pisgah**, Saranac Lake (www.saranaclakeny.gov); **Indian Lake Ski Hill** (http://townofindianlake.org); **Hickory Ski Center**, Warrensburg (www.hickoryskicenter.com); **Newcomb Ski Hill** (http://newcombny.com); and **Dynamite Hill**, Chestertown (www.townofchesterny.org).

Snowshoeing: Hundreds of miles of state-owned Forest Preserve lands are available for snowshoers in the Adirondacks.

Golf is one of the most popular pastimes in the Adirondacks, with public courses located throughout the Park. Contact your local information center for the closest links.

Birding: Bird watching in the Adirondack Park is an activity open to residents and visitors of all ages and abilities. Birding guides are available at your local gift shop/bookstore.

Rock/ice climbing: Outfitters, guides and sporting goods stores can help you find the nearest rock climbing opportunities, which are abundant in places such as the town of Keene, Essex County.

Mountain biking: There are a number of trails and back roads suitable for mountain biking; however, biking is restricted on certain state lands, such as Wilderness areas. The Whiteface Mountain region is a mountain biking paradise. Mountain biking with chairlift/gondola assistance is available in the summer at the Whiteface Mountain Ski Center, complete with rentals. The Wilmington Wild Trails System has 5 miles of trails in the Wilmington Wild Forest. There is also mountain biking at Gore Mountain in North Creek. Learn more at www.bikeadirondacks.org and www.whitefaceregion.com/recreation/biking.

Horseback riding: Equestrian trails are popular in many areas of the Park, even in the backcountry on state lands. The DEC may be able to help you find trails compatible for horses: www.dec.ny.gov.

Snowmobiling: There are thousands of miles of snowmobile trails in the Adirondack Mountains, and rail corridors and trails connect communities throughout the Adirondack Park. For a free Adirondack snowmobile map, contact the Adirondack Regional Tourism Council, P.O. Box 911, Lake Placid, NY 12946, (518) 846-8016.

Wild about the Park

Brook Trout Eat Breakfast, too

A proud native of our own Adirondacks, the brook trout is New York's official State Fish (how about that?) In fact, our waters contain genetically unique strains of brook trout: the tough Little Tupper Lake bunch has survived longer than others because it's resistant to the effects of acid rain.

Brook trout need cool, clean water year-round to survive. The best reason to love brook trout? Their favorite menu is black fly: tartare, flambeed, or baked for dinner, and river-bred freshly-laid eggs for breakfast. Scrambled. (But no coffee).

Find out more: contact AdirondackCouncil.org

Wild things happen in the Adirondacks.

ADIRONDACK
COUNCIL
www.AdirondackCouncil.org

INTERNATIONAL PAPER
www.internationalpaper.com

Hunter Safety

By MIKE MATTHEWS, DEC Sportsman Education Coordinator

All new hunters must attend a 10-hour hunter's safety course before they are allowed the privilege of hunting in New York. If these new sportsmen and sportswomen decide to bow hunt, they must take an additional eight-hour bowhunter education course. Interested in trapping? An eight-hour trapper education course is needed. The course work for the gun course includes wildlife management, hunting heritage, laws, firearm (shotgun, rifle, muzzleloader) handling and hunting ethics.

Follow these key hunting safety rules:
- Assume every gun is loaded
- Control the muzzle
- Finger off the trigger until ready to fire
- Be sure of the target and beyond
- Wear hunter orange

DEC has found that many hunting-related shooting incidents are associated with unlawful practices, such as shooting too close to a building. Finally, remember that 99.9 percent of the people who hunt have safe and enjoyable experiences. Over half a million people hunt in New York annually, and for every incident listed, there are thousands of other hunting stories of people who safely and responsibly took game. Just as important, even more passed up shots for the sake of safety, conservation and respect for wildlife.

Bicycling

Bicycling in the Adirondack Park provides adventures for all types of riders. Whether your preference is a long lakeside road tour, single track, fat-tire fun in the woods, a leisurely pedal down a lovely country road, or even a breakneck downhill dash at a ski center, the Park has it all.

Numerous bike shops throughout the region sponsor tours and events during the riding season. Regional chambers of commerce can be an excellent resource for additional information and referral. For those thrill seekers, several Adirondack ski areas provide downhill action and even lift service.

Many towns are developing mountain bike and multi-use trails on private or village lands. A simple Google search online can provide endless opportunities for exploration as well. For those seeking a more backcountry experience, it is important to note that use restrictions may apply on certain public lands.

Much of your road cycling on state land in the Park will be in Intensive Use areas (see NYS Forest Preserve). Wilderness is the most protective of the classifications, and no motorized vehicles or mountain bike use is permitted. The Wild Forest designation makes up over 1.3 million acres of the Forest Preserve, and the majority of trails in these areas allow mountain biking.

The same principles of Protect the Park and Protect Yourself that apply to other outdoor activities apply to cycling. Maintain adequate hydration and clothing, prepare and plan ahead, and leave nothing behind except tire tracks to denote your journeys.

Adirondack 46 High Peaks

The Adirondack Forty-Sixers are climbers who have climbed the 46 High Peaks of the Adirondacks with an elevation (generally) of 4,000 feet or more. In order to become a Forty-Sixer, a person must report these climbs in writing (no emails) to: The Office of the Historian, Adirondack Forty-Sixers, P.O. Box 9046, Schenectady, NY 12309.

MacNaughton (4,000 feet) gained Forty-Sixer stature with the most recent USGS survey. Although most Forty-Sixers climb it, it is not required. Information provided by www.adk46r.org.

Here are the 46 High Peaks (the "t" stands for trailless peak):

1 Marcy, 5,344	**24t** Seward, 4,361
2 Algonquin, 5,114	**25t** Marshall, 4,360
3 Haystack, 4,960	**26t** Allen, 4,340
4 Skylight, 4,926	**27** Big Slide, 4,240
5 Whiteface, 4,867	**28t** Esther, 4,240
6 Dix, 4,857	**29** Upper Wolf Jaw, 4,185
7t Gray, 4,840	**30** Lower Wolf Jaw, 4,175
8 Iroquois Peak, 4,840	**31t** Street, 4,166
9 Basin, 4,827	**32** Phelps, 4,161
10 Gothics, 4,736	**33t** Donaldson, 4,140
11 Colden, 4,714	**34t** Seymour, 4,120
12 Giant, 4,627	**35** Sawteeth, 4,100
13 Nippletop, 4,620	**36** Cascade, 4,098
14t Santanoni, 4,607	**37t** South Dix, 4,060
15t Redfield, 4,606	**38** Porter, 4,059
16 Wright Peak, 4,580	**39** Colvin, 4,057
17 Saddleback, 4,515	**40t** Emmons, 4,040
18t Panther, 4,442	**41** Dial, 4,020
19t TableTop, 4,427	**42t** East Dix, 4,012
20 Rocky Peak, 4,420	**43** Blake Peak, 3,960
21t Macomb, 4,405	**44t** Cliff, 3,960
22 Armstrong, 4,400	**45t** Nye, 3,895
23t Hough, 4,400	**46t** Couchsachraga, 3,820

Celebrating the High Peaks

To celebrate the 46 High Peaks, the Adirondack Mountain Club named 46 beds at the Adirondak Loj in Lake Placid after the peaks. And the Simply Gourmet restaurant on Saranac Avenue in Lake Placid, along with its sister restaurant on Main Street, the Creperie, have created 46 unique sandwiches named after the High Peaks.

Several Adirondack High Peaks, from left: Colden, Wright, Algonquin and Iroquois

Photo by Andy Flynn

Fish Creek Campground Photo

ANDY FLYNN

In other parts of the world, people live in tent communities because they've been displaced by war, famine or natural disaster. Here in the Adirondacks, it is part of tourism culture to live in a tent city for a weekend, a week or a month. Just go to Fish Creek.

After more than 90 years, the Fish Creek Pond State Campground in Franklin County continues to offer a safe haven for vacationers seeking solace in the great Adirondack wilderness. And even if the campground isn't quite wilderness as we know it, the throngs of campers don't seem to care.

They drive hundreds of miles to the mountains from places like New York City and Long Island, set up tents or campers within talking distance of one another, lay out picnic tablecloths, pile wood next to the fireplaces, poke around ice in the coolers for a refreshing beverage, and sit in their most comfortable folding chairs on the shoreline and around campfires, closing their eyes and forgetting the daily commute, leaving the maniacal Hutchinson River Parkway traffic to the worker bees too busy to visit Fish Creek in the Adirondacks.

I'll admit that car camping isn't my style. I'd rather be in a lean-to or a tent in the middle of the Forest Preserve. But I guess it's a matter of perspective. I drive by Knapp's Trading Post on state Route 30 (trying desperately to stick to the 35 mph limit in fear of stumbling upon a state police speed trap) and see the forested shoreline of Fish Creek Pond lined with tents and plumes of campfire smoke, and I see a tent city, a temporary community of campers larger than some hamlets in the Adirondacks. Faithful Fish Creek patrons, whose families have been camping here for decades, see something different. They see vacationland, a place to play, relax and make more memories for the kids and grandkids. And there's nothing wrong with that. It's a matter of perspective.

Car camping is currently one of the leading sectors in outdoor recreation in the United States, and it is an important part of the Adirondack economy. The Fish Creek Pond State Campground, attached at the hip with Rollins Pond State Campground, is the busiest state-run campground in the Adirondack Park. The state Department of Environmental Conservation (DEC) operates a total of 44 campgrounds in the Adirondack Park and eight in the Catskill Park.

The Adirondack Museum's exhibit, "The Great Outdoors: Adirondack Play & Adventure," highlights the popularity of car camping. A huge photo in the left-hand corner of the entryway, showing cars circa 1930 parked in campsites at Fish Creek Pond State Campground, spans two walls and is used as a backdrop for a camping display.

The photo is a gelatin silver print (a real photo postcard) and was produced by the Eastern Illustrating Co.

What strikes me about this photo, with vehicles parked under pine and birch trees along the dirt road, is the makeshift two-car garage that one family erected with tree poles and canvas material. I also noticed the platform tents, which Adirondack campers have used with decreasing popularity since the early 1970s.

New York state began constructing campsites in the Adirondacks in 1920, as more cars penetrated the Park on newly built roads. Road construction in the North Country was a frequent news topic in the Tupper Lake Herald in the early 1920s, as the increased mobility for travelers would be a boon to the village, which boasted two rail lines and a bustling logging/wood products industry at the time. At 10 miles driving distance, Tupper Lake is the closest village to Fish Creek, and many vacationers fondly remember their youthful days "camping in Tupper Lake."

In 1920, the state Conservation Commission set up a lean-to and a few fireplaces at Fish

Photo of the Fish Creek State Campground, circa 1930

Photo courtesy of the Adirondack Museum

Creek Pond to accommodate car campers, according to the DEC. The need for more sanitary facilities prompted growth at Fish Creek, where 20 campsites, sanitary facilities and a well were built in 1926. The amount of campsites was doubled in 1927 and doubled again in 1928.

"Although continually expanding, it was impossible to keep up with the demand for sites [at Fish Creek]," the DEC states on its website.

The Civilian Conservation Corps performed expansion duties at Fish Creek from 1933 to 1935. By the 1950s, demand increased so much that the state built an entirely new campground, Rollins Pond State Campground, to deal with the overflow of vacationers at Fish Creek. Rollins Pond opened in 1955 and was expanded in 1958 and 1960. It now has 287 campsites.

Today, there are 355 campsites at Fish Creek that offer room for tents to 40-foot recreational vehicles. The campground features a beach, playground, shower and bathroom facilities, boat launch, trailer dumping station, hiking trails, recreational and environmental education programs, boat and canoe rentals, and volleyball and basketball courts. The state has continued to spend hundreds of thousands of dollars renovating the campground and fixing erosion problems. Recent improvements have included the replacement of the water supply and sewage systems, the stabilization of shorelines at boat access locations and waterfront campsites, and campsite/facility upgrades to make the campground more accessible to people with disabilities.

The Fish Creek Pond State Campground also caters to early spring fishermen and late autumn hunters. With operating dates of mid-April to mid-November, it is typically the first state campground in all of New York to open for the season and the last to close.

(This story was first published in Andy Flynn's book, "New York State's Mountain Heritage: Adirondack Attic, Volume 3.")

Camping in the Adirondacks

DEC STAFF

There are countless opportunities to camp in the Adirondack Park, whether it's bivouacked in the deep woods alone, tent camping or sleeping in a lean-to on state land, bunking in a backwoods cabin, or parking an RV at a campground. There are a number of excellent privately owned campgrounds in the Adirondack Park.

The Department of Environmental Conservation operates 42 campgrounds located in the Adirondack Park. DEC campgrounds provide a wide variety of experiences, including island camping, tent and trailer camping, boat launching facilities, hiking trails, beaches and day use areas with picnic tables and grills. Learn more at www.dec.ny.gov.

Bears: The DEC encourages the use of bear-resistant canisters throughout the Adirondack and Catskill backcountry. Bear-resistant canisters are required to be used by overnight users in the Eastern High Peaks Wilderness between April 1 and Nov. 30.

Firewood: A regulation is in effect prohibiting the import of firewood into New York unless it has been heat-treated to kill forest pests and pathogens. The regulation also limits the transportation of untreated firewood to less than 50 miles from its source. It is best to leave all firewood at home. Get your firewood at the campground or from a local vendor — ask for a receipt or label that has the firewood's local source. More details at www.dec.ny.gov/animals/28722.html.

Backcountry camping: Backcountry camping is allowed on Forest Preserve lands in the Adirondacks. Specific land units in the Forest Preserve may have regulations that differ from the rules and guidelines listed below. For information about specific land areas, look at the DEC regulations page (www.dec.ny.gov) or contact the regional office near the land unit of interest.

Mud-season hiking: Avoid high-elevation trails

With the start of a new season of outdoor hiking and recreation on public lands in the Adirondacks, hikers are anxious to climb mountains before blackflies and other biting insects become prevalent.

However, high-elevation trails are wet and muddy during the spring, making them vulnerable to degradation from hikers. The best thing a hiker can do for the high-elevation trails and plant communities is to postpone taking any hikes on trails above 3,000 feet until mid-June, when the trails have dried and hardened. Hikers are advised to only use trails at lower elevations during the spring mud season, to avoid damaging natural resources and promote safety. Lower trails usually dry soon after snowmelt and are on less erosive soils than the higher peaks.

High-elevation trails in the Dix, Giant, and High Peaks Wilderness Areas of the northern Adirondacks are particularly vulnerable.

Remember when hiking in wet and muddy conditions to wear waterproof footwear and gaiters and walk through — not around — mud and water on trails. This will avoid unnecessary trampling of vegetation and widening of trails.

Check the New York State Department of Environmental Conservation website contains additional information on trail conditions in the Adirondacks (http://www.dec.ny.gov/outdoor/7865.html) or you may contact the DEC Forest Rangers at (518) 897-1300.

Lean-to camping along the Raquette River, Hamilton County
Photo by Andy Flynn

Backcountry camping guidelines: Rules and guidelines for the use of public lands managed by DEC are generally as follows:

•Camping is prohibited within 150 feet of any road, trail, spring, stream, pond or other body of water except at areas designated by a "camp here" disk.

•Groups of 10 or more persons, or stays of more than three days in one place, require a permit from the local Forest Ranger.

•Lean-tos are available in many areas on a first come, first served basis. Lean-tos cannot be used exclusively and must be shared with other campers.

•Use pit privies provided near popular camping areas and trailheads. If none are available, dispose of human waste by digging a hole 6-8 inches deep at least 150 feet from water or campsites. Cover the hole with leaves and soil.

•Don't use soap to wash yourself, clothing or dishes within 150 ft of water.

•Drinking and cooking water should be boiled for 5 minutes, treated with purifying tablets or filtered through filtration device to prevent instances of giardia infection.

•Fires should be built in existing fire pits or fireplaces if provided. Use only dead and down wood for fires. Cutting standing trees is prohibited. Extinguish all fires with water, and stir ashes until they are cold to the touch. Do not build fires in areas marked by a "No Fires" disk. Camp stoves are safer, more efficient and cleaner.

•Carry out what you carry in. Practice "leave no trace" camping.

•Keep your pet under control. Restrain it on a leash when others approach. Collect and bury droppings away from water, trails and camp sites. Keep your pet away from drinking water sources.

•Observe and enjoy wildlife and plants, but leave them undisturbed.

•Removing plants, rocks, fossils or artifacts from state land without a permit is illegal.

•The storage of personal property on state land is prohibited.

•Carry an approved personal flotation device for each person aboard all watercraft.

•Except in an emergency or between Dec. 15 and April 30, camping is prohibited above an elevation of 4,000 feet in the Adirondacks.

•At all times, only emergency fires are permitted above 4,000 feet in the Adirondacks.

Adirondack Forest Preserve Map

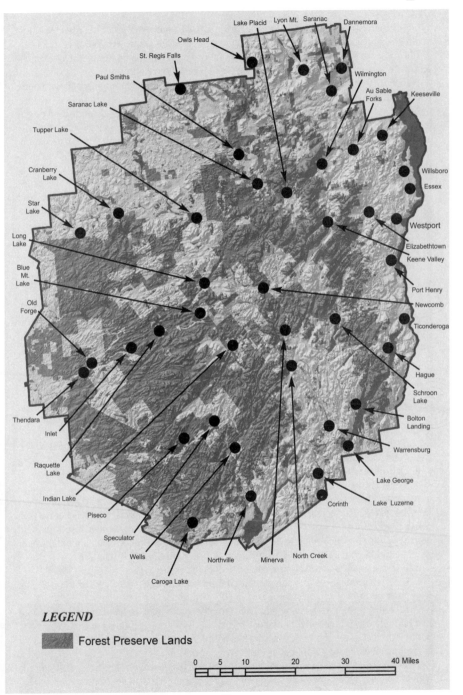

LEGEND

Forest Preserve Lands

0 5 10 20 30 40 Miles

Fishing in the Adirondacks

DEC STAFF

Good anglers respect the Adirondack Park's water resources in order to protect wildlife and their habitat as well as to protect the sport of fishing for future generations.

Plan Ahead: Know and follow fishing regulations and be prepared to care for your catch. Know the weather forecast and take PFDs (life jacket). Leave a trip plan.

Never Litter: This includes old fishing line (including line trimmings), food wrappers, bait containers, empty cans or bottles and plastic bags.

Non-Toxic Sinkers: Lost sinkers, especially split-shot, may be mistaken for food or grit and eaten by waterfowl such as ducks, geese, swans, gulls or loons. Toxic effects of even a single lead sinker can cause birds to sicken and increase the risk of death through predation, exposure or lead poisoning. The sale of certain lead sinkers (including "split shot") weighing one-half ounce or less is prohibited in New York state.

Nesting Birds: Many species of birds select nest sites on or close to water. These include ducks, geese, swans, loons, herons, ospreys and eagles. Close approach by boaters and anglers may cause these birds to leave their nests. This makes the eggs or young vulnerable to predators, chilling, overheating and possible abandonment and starvation.

Catch and Release: Fish populations are a limited resource, and anglers can have an impact on the quality of these populations. Consider these catch-and-release practices.

1. Quickly play and land fish.
2. Have necessary tools on hand to remove the hook.
3. Unhook fish in the water if possible.
4. Handle fish carefully to avoid injury — avoid contact with gills. Do not squeeze fish or remove protective slime. Do not grasp fish by the eye sockets. Do not hold large northern pike or musky in a vertical position as this can damage internal organs — handle/hold them horizontally.
5. Cut leaders on deeply hooked fish.
6. Consider using barbless or circle hooks.
7. Don't "cull" by killing fish considered undesirable.

Guidelines to prevent the spread of Aquatic Invasive Species

1. Remove all sediment and aquatic plants from all recreational gear including boots, waders, nets, boats, motors and trailers before departing an access site.
2. Drain all water from your boat before leaving the launch or access site, including bilges, live-wells and bait tanks.
3. Dry all fishing gear such as nets and boots before traveling to another water body.
4. Consider disinfecting live wells. Use a 1-2 percent chlorine/water solution (3 ounces of household bleach per gallon of water) to kill organisms, particularly after entering known infected waters. Rinse gear well after treatment to remove all residual chlorine before next reuse. Do not let rinse water enter lakes or streams. NOTE: 10 percent bleach solution will destroy waders and electronic wiring. Wader disinfection is best done using either hot water or by spraying with a household disinfectant such as Formula 409 or Fantastic.
5. Use responsible live-well procedures to avoid stressing fish.
6. Use certified disease-free bait purchased from licensed bait dealers. Keep the sales slip from your bait to show it was purchased legally within the last seven days.
7. It is illegal to: transport any live fish from one water body to another; release unused live bait into any water body; or dispose of fish carcasses or byproducts in any water body within 100 feet of the shoreline. NOTE: It is not illegal to dispose of fish carcasses in water — you just have to do it 100 feet or more away from shore.

Pack out fish waste: Ideally take fish home to clean them. In the field, fish entrails should be buried at least 6 inches deep and 150 feet from water, trails or campsites.

Fishing on the Raquette River, which flows from Raquette Lake north to the St. Lawrence River.

Photo by Andy Flynn

'Assaulted by Mosquitoes' Photo

ANDY FLYNN

The look on Mr. Brandt's face says it all. He appears to be exhausted as he sits, surrendering to the onslaught of biting insects, on a rock in front of a wilderness lean-to in the southwestern Adirondacks. This is the daze of "bug season." All you can do is cover up and swat like a madman until you're so tired that you finally give up and simply become another mammal in the woods. Just when you've climbed to the top of the food chain, you're humbled by swarms of blackflies, deer flies, no-see-ums and mosquitoes. Today, in the Adirondack forest, you are food.

The "Woods and Waters: Outdoor Recreation in the Adirondacks" exhibit at the Adirondack Museum showcases the effects of biting insects on the brave souls who venture into the woods for a little hiking, camping, fishing, etc. A single display, accompanied by a looped recording of historical quotes from authors describing their adventures during bug season, features a bug hat, a collection of various homemade and store-bought insect repellents, and a whiskey bottle. Apparently, the insects drove many to drink.

On the wall, above the bottles of bug dope, is the photograph of Mr. Brandt. The title is "Battle for Life: Mr. Brandt Assaulted by Mosquitoes," Pine Hill Camp, Moose River, about 1894. The man is certainly not smiling. I'm not sure when photographers began telling their subjects to "Say cheese," but Mr. Brandt probably would not have given his photographer the satisfaction of a bright and cheery smile at this particular moment. He looks uncomfortable, dressed in long pants, a long-sleeved jacket over a shirt and vest, and a hat. He also has cloth wrapped around his head, protecting his chin, ears and forehead. Very little skin is showing.

It has long been said that there are two seasons in the Adirondack Mountains: winter and the Fourth of July. In reality, we have at least six by my estimate, including spring, summer, fall and winter. There are two sub-seasons in spring: mud season and bug season. Bug season is usually associated with blackflies, which hatch in the swift-running streams while the snow is melting. When does bug season begin and end? That's tough to say, and it varies depending where you live inside the Park. It's safe to say that the peak of bug season is mid-May to late June. That's primarily when the blackflies are most abundant; however, mosquitoes, deer flies and no-see-ums are tenacious throughout the summer, and blackflies don't just disappear. You'll see biting insects until the snow flies, but they are not as bad in the second half of the summer when leaves start changing and nights get cooler.

There are several factors that affect the length of bug season, including the weather. Long periods of warm, dry weather in May will decrease the amount of blackflies. It will also bring out the deer flies early. Generally, blackfly season begins about two weeks after the ice goes out. During the first week of the season, the blackflies are "drunk" and disoriented. Then they get organized and begin biting in earnest. And no matter how many clothes you have on your body, they will find a way to get to your skin: in socks, up pants legs, in ears, up noses, in hair, up your shirt. At night, sleeping in a lean-to in mid-June in the deepest wilds of the Adirondacks, it is torturous. If the blackflies don't get you, the mosquitoes will. So, if you're going to camp during the spring and first half of summer, sleep in a tent. Leave the romance of an open camp to the miserable.

The Rev. William H.H. "Adirondack" Murray tried to dispel the myth of the blackfly in his 1869 bestseller, "Adventures in the Wilderness." He asserted that blackflies were unfairly demonized by the media:

"I regard it as one of the most harmless and least vexatious of the insect family. For five years my wife and self have camped in the wilderness; we have traversed it near and far,

Mr. Brandt

Photo courtesy of the Adirondack Museum

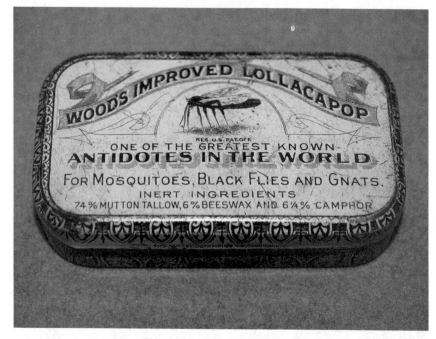

Tin of Wood's Improved Lollacapop
Photo courtesy of the Adirondack Museum

sleeping where the night found us, but we have never been, to any extent worth mentioning, disturbed by its presence. The black fly, as pictured by 'our Adirondack correspondent,' like the Gorgon of old, is a myth, — a monster existing only in men's feverish imaginations."

A special correspondent, Wachusett, took issue with Murray's exaggerations and disregard for the blackfly in a set of Adirondack-based articles in July 1869 in the Boston Daily Advertiser:

"I have spoken of the prevalence of the mosquitoes. With these must be included the black flies. Either these insects have not read Mr. Murray's book, or they have mislaid their almanac; or, what is more probable, the lateness and wetness of the season has prolonged their term of life; for certainly the first week of July finds them here in undiminished numbers."

Wachusett did not contradict Murray, regarding blackflies, but he reported on some insect incidents that helped set the record straight:

"I have seen parties hurrying back to the haunts of men from camps which they had sought but a few days before with high hopes of pleasure, driven away solely and simply by the stings of these little torments ... I have seen a gentleman so disfigured by mosquitoes that he sought a resting place where his bites might heal before he would present himself to his friends."

Perhaps Mr. Brandt experienced similar bug season nightmares along the Moose River in the 1890s. Perhaps you are living through it right now.

(This story was first published in Andy Flynn's book, "New York State's Mountain Heritage: Adirondack Attic, Volume 6.")

Bug Dope in the Adirondacks

ANDY FLYNN

Knowing the bug basics — when and where they are abundant and what type of weather they are most active — is one thing. Stopping the blackflies, mosquitoes, deerflies and no-see-ums from biting is quite another.

Ask around the Adirondacks for tips. Everyone has at least one. Dress in light-colored clothing. Use such-and-such bug spray. Eat a lot of garlic. Don't go outside until the snow flies. It seems man has been collecting bug-prevention remedies since the dawn of time.

I've heard my fair share of tips. One friend says use bug dope with as much DEET as possible. Another says put a fern in your hat, and let it hover over your head like a halo, so the deerflies fly to the top of the fern instead of biting you behind the ears. Many people are content with over-the-counter sprays and lotions. In the summer, you can track tourists by smell on the trails; they bathe in the stuff. Kids are told to close their eyes and mouths as Deep Woods OFF is sprayed on every exposed piece of skin. Women, looking to drive away the bugs and condition their skin at the same time, swore that Avon Skin So Soft was a miracle repellant long before the company extended its brand to Skin So Soft Bug Guard.

I remember growing up in Tupper Lake in the late 1970s when airplanes sprayed neighborhoods with bug-killing spray, parents yelling at their kids to get inside the house, afraid they'd get poisoned and die of cancer. Then towns such as North Elba in Essex County began treating their streams with BTI to kill blackfly larvae so the golfers in Lake Placid wouldn't complain about the abundance of bugs and travel elsewhere.

I don't use bug dope. It doesn't work for me, and that's fine because I don't like putting chemicals all over my body. Instead, I wear a hat and try to keep moving when taking a hike in the woods. When sleeping in a lean-to, I wear a winter hat and mittens while in my sleeping bag, even in the summer, to leave as little skin exposed as possible. I've finally learned to sleep in a tent most of the time. I figure, if I'm going to spend time in the backcountry, bugs are part of the experience, part of the landscape. I might as well get over it and make sure I pack some Calamine lotion.

Nineteenth century Adirondack literature is filled with stories about biting insects and ways to repel them. Some are adaptable to today's camper, and others are antiquated. The old writers also used some different names for the popular Adirondack bugs. No-see-ums, for example, were also called gnats, midges and punkies.

In his 1872 book, "Modern Babes in the Wood: Or Summerings in the Wilderness," H. Perry Smith had more choice words for punkies than any other Adirondack bug:

"They can drill a hole in a person's skin twice as deep as their own bodies are long, in just two-fifths of a second, eat a square meal of his blood and get away in another fifth, digest it and return hungry during the other two."

And that's just one no-see-um. What about a swarm of them?

"We despair of giving you an adequate description of the sensations experienced from an attack of a well regulated family of punkies, but it may be likened to a constant shower of fine sharp sand upon one's face, each grain of which should be poisoned sufficiently to leave a sting for five minutes."

Location, location, location. In order to minimize the bug-biting experience, the Rev. William H.H. "Adirondack" Murray suggested that people put more thought into the location of their camping site. His 1869 bestseller, "Adventures in the Wilderness," detailed the best location of a campsite:

"A headland, or a point which projects into a lake, over which the wind sweeps, or, better still, an island, is excellent ground for a camp, where mosquitoes will not embarrass you."

Murray also told campers to cover up their skin, even their hands, sewing on an armlet or a gauntlet of chamois-skin to a pair of buckskin gloves. This covered the hands and arms all the way up to the elbow. And, if they created a head net of Swiss mull and an elastic band, attached to a collar, "you can laugh defiance at the mosquitoes and gnats."

Smudges were popular ways to get rid of all kinds of bugs. Bugs don't like smoke, so build a fire with damp and/or green wood and create as much smoke as possible. Murray suggested smoking a "very fine" piece of muslin, hanging it at the doorway, "and behind its protection sleep undisturbed."

"Punkies can't live in thick smoke," Smith wrote in 1872, "but the trouble with this remedy is that there are but few men who can live many days and breathe nothing else."

Applying ointment to the skin was the most widely distributed remedy. Murray used a bottle of sweet oil and a vial of tar, applying it to his face.

"All manner of insects abhor the smell of tar," Murray wrote in 1869. "To reconcile my lady readers to it, I may add, that it renders the skin soft and smooth as the infant's."

Smith wasn't too keen on the "Oil of Tar" method:

"If punkies show any good taste or discrimination, it is in their unwillingness to suck blood through a coating of that stuff. It makes a man smell like the ruins after a fire, and his face look like a smoked shoulder."

Smith's clean, sweet-smelling alternative was to apply pennyroyal oil, mixed with fresh lard. This, in addition to the operation of a smudge to "clear a tent or shanty before retiring," was his solution.

Seneca Ray Stoddard, in his 1878 issue of Adirondacks Illustrated, subscribed to the bug remedies of those before him, offering Murray's suggestion of choosing a wind-swept camping spot, smudging out the bugs in the tent before going to bed, placing a sheet of thin

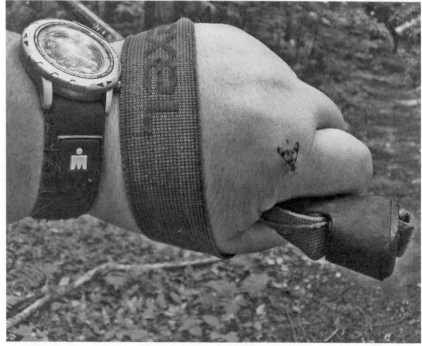

Deer fly biting the author's hand

Photo by Andy Flynn

Blackfly biting the author's arm

muslin at the tent's entrance, and wearing extended gloves and a Swiss muslin bag over the head. Plus, he suggested two bug dopes: mutton tallow (six ounces) mixed with pennyroyal (one ounce) and a touch of camphor; and a solution of sweet oil and tar.

An old homemade bottle of "Essence of Fly-Dope," found in the "Woods and Waters: Outdoor Recreation in the Adirondacks" exhibit at the Adirondack Museum, shows a label with the ingredients: "Oil of Tar (3) oil of Pennyroyal (2) / (Mix for use with Raw Linseed Oil in proportion of three to seven)."

Then there were mass-marketed bug lotions. The exhibit also includes a small yellow tin of Woods Improved Lollacapop, "one of the greatest known antidotes in the world for mosquitoes, black flies and gnats." It was made of 74 percent mutton tallow, 6 percent beeswax and 6.25 percent camphor. It does not state what is in the remaining 13.75 percent of the mixture.

In his 1884 book, "Woodcraft," George Washington Sears (a.k.a. Nessmuk), repeats Murray's suggestions for battling the bugs; however, he offered a personal solution he had been using for more than 40 years: 3 ounces of pine tar, 2 ounces of castor oil and 1 ounce of pennyroyal. He boiled it together and then bottled it, only needing a 2-ounce vial the entire summer season. Why did he need so little ointment? You wouldn't need much either if you never washed up. Rub it into your skin until there is a good glaze, like varnishing a piece of furniture, and add a little more each day. In 1883, Nessmuk carried a cake of soap and a towel in his pack for seven weeks and didn't use it once:

"When I had established a good glaze on the skin, it was too valuable to be sacrificed for any weak whim connected with soap and water ... I found the mixture gave one's face the ruddy tanned look supposed to be indicative of health and hard muscle."

Nessmuk waited until he reached a hotel in order to wash up in the public wash basin.

(This story was first published in Andy Flynn's book, "New York State's Mountain Heritage: Adirondack Attic, Volume 6.")

Essentials for Hiking & Camping

Ten Essentials

1. Map
2. Compass
3. Flashlight/headlamp (be sure to have an extra set of batteries that fit your flashlight/headlamp)
4. Extra food (enough for one extra day)
5. Extra clothing
6. Rain gear (jacket and pants) Always carry rain gear, even if the sun is out.
7. First-aid supplies (be sure to include an extra day of any medication you are taking or might need in an emergency)
8. Pocket knife
9. Matches (stored in a water-tight container in addition to matches or a butane lighter)
10. Fire starter (can be candles, chemical fire starter, backpack-size fire logs)

Other Essentials

•Space blanket (used as windbreaker, heat reflector, signaling device)
•Sunglasses
•Toilet paper
•Extra socks/liners
•Head covering (for rain/warmth)
•Duct tape
•Insect repellent
•Iodine tablets or water pump (carry extra water if water location is a potential problem)
•Trash bag
•"In case of emergency" card

   a) List a name and number to call in an emergency, medications, medical conditions and whether you are a contact lenses wearer.

   b) Pack your driver's license and insurance card in a plastic bag for protection.

Island camping on Middle Saranac Lake, Franklin County

Photo by Andy Flynn

Wild about the Park

Songbirds that Winter in the Carribean & Summer in the Adirondacks?

Humans aren't the only ones that summer in the Adirondacks. Meet Bicknell's Thrush, a rare, elusive songbird which breeds -- and summers -- in the Adirondack mountaintop spruce and fir at over 3000 feet. (And doesn't get dizzy, even belting out Sinatra.)

In the winters, however, these songbird snowbirds can be found in the Caribbean. Nope, we're not whistling Dixie. The Adirondack Council and partners are working to preserve their lands there, too. (Wouldn't it be nice for all of us to share a concert with one come Adirondack wintertime.)

Find out more: contact AdirondackCouncil.org

Wild things happen in the Adirondacks.

ADIRONDACK
COUNCIL
www.AdirondackCouncil.org

INTERNATIONAL PAPER
www.internationalpaper.com

Natural History Illustration by Sheri Amsel www.exploringnature.org

Backcountry Preparedness

DEC STAFF

Backcountry hiking trails can be rugged and rough — they are not maintained as park walkways — wear proper footwear. Wilderness conditions can change suddenly. If bad weather sets in or you become physically distressed, turn back.

All users should plan accordingly, including bringing flashlight, first-aid equipment, extra food and clothing. Weather conditions may alter your plans; you should always be prepared to spend an unplanned night in the woods before entering the backcountry.

Properly plan and prepare.

Know
•Your own physical capabilities, knowledge of backcountry recreation and skill level
•The distance you plan to travel and the terrain and conditions you will encounter

Check
•Local forest ranger for current information.
•Current weather conditions and short-term forecast

Wear
•Appropriate outerwear and footwear (waterproof boots, gaiters and waterproof outerwear)
•Layers of non-cotton clothes

Carry
•Map and compass — know how to use them … and use them
•Flashlight and extra batteries
•Plenty of food and water

Pack
•Extra clothes and socks
•Hat and gloves or mittens
•Ensolite pad to rest on and insulate your body from cold surfaces
•Bivy sack or space blankets for extra warmth
•Fire starter supplies: waterproof matches, butane lighter, candles, starter material, etc.

Estimate a reasonable time of arrival at the destination and turn back at that time even if you haven't reached your destination.

Always inform someone of your itinerary and when you expect to return.

Report backcountry emergencies, such as lost or injured hikers, and wildland fires to the DEC forest rangers at (518) 891-0235.

Sagamore Lake in the town of Long Lake, Hamilton County

Photo by Andy Flynn

Sign in the Saranac Lakes Wild Forest, Franklin County

Photo by Andy Flynn

NYS Forest Preserve

DEC and APA STAFF

New York state has one of the oldest land preservation programs in the U.S. New Yorkers established the Forest Preserve as an act of the Legislature in 1885, declaring that state-owned lands in eight Adirondack and three Catskill counties should "be forever kept as wild forest lands." Further, the land could not be sold or leased. In 1892, the Adirondack Park was created to encompass both the Forest Preserve and private lands in the region. The state Constitution, updated in 1894, redefined the Forest Preserve, adding that lands shall not be cut, "nor shall the timber thereon be sold, removed, or destroyed."

Currently, there are 2.7 million acres of Forest Preserve lands in the Adirondacks. The Department of Environmental Conservation, under state law, has "care, custody and control" of the Forest Preserve lands.

The Adirondack Park State Land Master Plan, overseen by the Adirondack Park Agency, identifies the various management units of the Forest Preserve, assigns each of the units a land classification category and provides the guidelines for management and recreation for each classification. The following state land classification definitions are from the Adirondack Park State Land Master Plan. The second part of each definition is provided by the DEC and explains what kind of recreational activities are allowed.

See an Adirondack Park Map with the state Forest Preserve lands on the DEC website at http://www.dec.ny.gov/docs/lands_forests_pdf/adkmap.pdf.

Wilderness

A wilderness area, in contrast with those areas where man and his own works dominate the landscape, is an area where the earth and its community of life are untrammeled by man — where man himself is a visitor who does not remain. A wilderness area is further defined to mean an area of state land or water having a primeval character, without significant improvement or permanent human habitation, which is protected and managed so as to preserve, enhance and restore, where necessary, its natural conditions, and which (1) generally appears to have been affected primarily by the forces of nature, with the imprint of man's work substantially unnoticeable; (2) has outstanding opportunities for solitude or a primitive and unconfined type of recreation; (3) has at least ten thousand acres of contiguous land and water or is of sufficient size and character as to make practicable its preservation and use in an unimpaired condition; and (4) may also contain ecological, geological or other features of scientific, educational, scenic or historical value.

Wilderness Recreation: 18 Forest Preserve units, containing approximately 1.1 million acres of land, are classified as "Wilderness." Recreational activities on wilderness lands and waters is limited to non-motorized recreation such as hiking, hunting, fishing, primitive camping, rock climbing, swimming, skiing, snowshoeing, canoeing and kayaking. Motorized vehicles, motorized boats and mountain biking are prohibited on wilderness lands. Except in very rare cases, the only structures or facilities permitted on these lands are lean-tos, primitive tent sites, trails, foot bridges and pit privies.

Primitive

A primitive area is an area of land or water that is either:

1. Essentially wilderness in character but, (a) contains structures, improvements, or uses that are inconsistent with wilderness, as defined, and whose removal, though a long term objective, cannot be provided for by a fixed deadline, and/or, (b) contains, or is contiguous to, private lands that are of a size and influence to prevent wilderness designation; or,

2. Of a size and character not meeting wilderness standards, but where the fragility of the resource or other factors require wilderness management.

Primitive Recreation: 11 Forest Preserve units larger than 1,000 acres, and more than 20 corridors or other small pieces, totaling approximately 66,000 acres, are classified as "Primitive." Primitive areas are managed the same as wilderness areas and recreational activities are restricted to those allowed on lands and waters classified as wilderness. (The tracts classified "Primitive rather than "Wilderness" because of substantial privately owned "in-holdings" or structures that don't conform with wilderness guidelines.) The primitive corridors are typically public or private roads within a wilderness area, if it is public road, cars and trucks are allowed on them.

Canoe

A canoe area is an area where the watercourses or the number and proximity of lakes and ponds make possible a remote and unconfined type of water-oriented recreation in an essentially wilderness setting.

Canoe Area Recreation: Only one Forest Preserve unit, the 18,000-acre St. Regis Canoe Area, is classified as a "Canoe Area." Canoe areas are managed as wilderness areas, with a focus on non-motorized, water-based activities such as canoeing, kayaking and fishing. Primitive camping is allowed at sites accessible only by water. Mountain biking is allowed on the administrative roads.

Wild Forest

A wild forest area is an area where the resources permit a somewhat higher degree of human use than in wilderness, primitive or canoe areas, while retaining an essentially wild character. A wild forest area is further defined as an area that frequently lacks the sense of remoteness of wilderness, primitive or canoe areas and that permits a wide variety of outdoor recreation.

Wild Forest Recreation: 20 Forest Preserve units, containing approximately 1.3 million acres of land, are classified as "Wild Forest." A wider variety of recreational activities are allowed on the lands and waters in wild forest areas. In addition to the recreational activities allowed on wilderness lands and waters, some forms of motorized recreation are allowed with restrictions. Cars and trucks may only drive on designated roads; snowmobiles may only use designated trails and roads; mountain bikes can use any trails or roads unless prohibited by signs and some specific waters have restrictions on the horsepower of a boat's motor, allow the use of electric motors only or may be prohibit any motors. Drive-up campsites are provided along some roadways in wild forests areas.

Intensive Use

An intensive use area is an area where the state provides facilities for intensive forms of outdoor recreation by the public. Two types of intensive use areas are defined by this plan: campground and day use areas. There are 42 campgrounds, 25 boat launches, six day-use areas and two ski centers owned by the state in the Adirondack Park. These areas provide for recreational activities like group camping, swimming, boating, picnicking and skiing.

Historic

Historic areas are locations of buildings, structures or sites owned by the state (other than the Adirondack Forest Preserve itself) that are significant in the history, architecture, archeology or culture of the Adirondack Park, the state or the nation; that fall into one of the following categories; state historic sites; properties listed on the National Register of Historic Places; and properties recommended for nomination by the Committee on Registers of the New York State Board For Historic Preservation; and that are of a scale, character and location appropriate for designation as an historic area under this master plan and the state has committed resources to manage such areas primarily for historic objectives.

State Administrative

State administrative areas are areas where the state provides facilities for a variety of specific state purposes that are not primarily designed to accommodate visitors to the Park.

Conservation Easement

Currently there are more than 750,000 acres of privately owned lands in the Adirondack Park which the state owns development rights, and often public recreation rights, called "Conservation Easement Lands." Typically, these lands are owned and/or managed by timber companies, but the ability to subdivide and build structures on these lands are prohibited or severely limited. The public recreation rights on these lands range from no public access, to access limited to specific corridors or locations, to full public recreation rights. The recreation activities on these lands can be restricted by type, location and season. Check with the Department of Environmental Conservation to learn what recreational activities are allowed on specific parcels. DEC State land regulations apply on any conservation easement land that has public recreational rights.

Easements in the Park (county)

- Croghan Tract (Lewis)
- Long Pond Conservation Easement (St. Lawrence)
- Oswegatchie Easement Lands (Lewis, Herkimer, St. Lawrence)
- Paul Smith's College Conservation Easement (Franklin)
- Perkins Clearing/Speculator Tree Farm Conservation Easement Lands (Hamilton)
- Sable Highlands Conservation Easement Lands (Clinton, Franklin)
- Santa Clara Tract Conservation Easement Lands (Franklin, St. Lawrence)
- Tooley Pond Tract (St. Lawrence)
- Upper Hudson Woodlands Conservation Easement (Essex, Fulton, Hamilton, Saratoga, Warren)

Special Notes

Other than on intensive use areas, the Forest Preserve lands are designed and managed to emphasize the self-sufficiency of the recreational users. When recreating on the Forest Preserve, you must assume a high degree of responsibility for environmentally sound use of such areas and for your own health, safety and welfare.

Be sure to know the laws and regulations governing a recreational activity before participating in that activity.

Horseback riding is allowed on roads open for public use, trails that are marked for horse use, and trails marked for skiing or snowmobiling when there is no snow or ice on the ground.

All-Terrain Vehicles (ATVs) are prohibited on all Forest Preserve lands.

Recreational activities on the approximately 2.9 million acres of private lands within the Adirondack Park, not under a conservation easement, are not restricted any more than activities on private lands throughout the rest of the state. The public is prohibited from entering private lands without permission of the landowner.

Contact the Department of Environmental Conservation Lands & Forests office for more information: Region 5 (518-897-1291) or Region 6 (315-785-2261).

Forest Preserve Education

The **Adirondack Forest Preserve Education Partnership (AFPEP)** seeks to protect the Adirondack Forest Preserve and other publicly accessible lands and waters by educating people about these resources and how to safely enjoy and protect them.

AFPEP provides current information pertaining to natural resource conservation, low impact recreation and appropriate use of the Forest Preserve. It seeks to reduce the negative effects of overuse and abuse by informing users about pressing ecological issues and responsible recreational practices.

Additionally, AFPEP provides information to avoid conflicts between users, especially people participating in different forms of recreation. It reinforces the idea that everyone can enjoy the Adirondacks, no matter what type of recreation they participate in.

AFPEP is an unincorporated group of partner organizations from the Adirondacks which includes the Adirondack Mountain Club, Wildlife Conservation Society, Adirondack Park Invasive Plant Program, Adirondack Regional Tourism Council, Leading Edge and the New York State Department of Environmental Conservation.

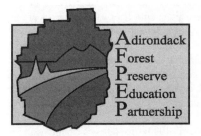
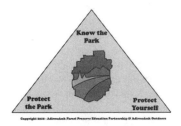

Why 'Adirondack Outdoors'?

The Adirondack Park has something for everyone. With 2.5 million acres of Forest Preserve public land and another 3.5 million acres of private land, recreational activities are available for the entire range of outdoor enthusiasts. Whether you like to paddle on a quiet pond or motorboat across the large expanses of open water, whether you like to ski the backcountry or snowmobile the 1,800 miles of trails that wind through the park, whether you like to hunt small or large game or are a birder in search of another sighting to add to your life list, the Adirondack Forest Preserve has recreational activities for you.

This publication is designed, in part, to help you make sure you have a safe, enjoyable recreational experience and protect this unique resource we call the Forest Preserve for future generations of visitors and residents. Much of the information focuses on three elements:
- Knowing about the Park;
- Protecting Yourself; and
- Protecting the Park.

It is only through the awareness of these topics and the skills to implement them that we can be sure to preserve the opportunities to participate in these activities and minimize their regulation.

Buck Lake Club Camp

ANDY FLYNN

When the state of New York buys vast tracts of land in the Adirondack Park, or purchases easement rights, it opens up thousands of acres of forest to the public for recreational opportunities. It also prevents development at key environmental locations, especially along the shorelines of backcountry lakes and rivers. But, as some natives assert, there are casualties in this "land grab," and a way of life is slowly disappearing.

You see, paper manufacturers and other private companies own some of these tracts, and they lease out the land to hunting and fishing clubs to help pay the taxes. When the taxes get too high, they sell the land or easements on the land to New York state through a middle-man organization such as the Adirondack Nature Conservancy. Many of these clubs, and their backwoods cabins, are subsequently kicked off the land they've been leasing for generations. All of a sudden, goin' upta camp ain't what it used to be.

When the state bought more than 16,000 acres of land from International Paper Co. in the Herkimer County town of Webb in 1986, in the far northern corner called Watson's East Triangle, a way of life began disappearing for many hunters in that region. Most lived in nearby Lewis County to the west. The club members were given until Sept. 10, 1991 to clear out, taking their structures with them or leaving them for the state to burn.

The tract was to become state Forest Preserve in what is now part of the 13,229-acre Watson's East Triangle Wild Forest. It was to become a playground for the public, with ample opportunities for hunting, fishing, trapping, hiking and snowmobiling. The Middle Branch of the Oswegatchie River runs through it, and the West Branch of the Oswegatchie begins its journey north from a small body of water in the Triangle, at a place called Buck Pond.

It was here at Buck Pond, in the late 1980s and early 1990s, that a Lewis County man became a folk hero for standing up to the state of New York, defiantly fighting for his right to keep the hunting cabin he built with his family and friends in the early 1960s. He lost the battle, taking the last of his belongings out of camp in the late summer of 1991, leaving heart broken and angry.

Michael C. Virkler, of Castorland, was 85 when the state officially banned non-conforming structures from the Forest Preserve in the Watson's East Triangle on Sept. 10, 1991. But the DEC didn't burn Virkler's hunting cabin, known as the Buck Lake Club camp, as Virkler thought they would. Instead, DEC officials looked for options to save the log cabin, and they eventually moved it, piece by piece, to the Adirondack Museum in Blue Mountain Lake.

"We recognize that's a pretty unique structure and certainly worthy of preservation," DEC Region 6 Director Thomas E. Brown told Watertown Daily Times Staff Writer John Golden for a Nov. 6, 1988 article. "The last thing I think any of us would want to see is to see that razed or destroyed. I think we can work something out."

And they did. In February 1992, DEC staff, Virkler and Adirondack Museum employee Mark K. Schisler took apart the 18-by-24-foot cabin and hauled it out of Watson's East Triangle. All the logs were marked, as were almost 200 stones from the fireplace, and re-assembled at the Adirondack Museum in the following years.

This is a unique cabin because it was constructed without any nails or spikes. Gravity, dovetail joints, tongue-and-groove cuts, and round, wooden pegs held it together. It was a work of art, and Virkler was the craftsman.

Virkler and his wife, Hilda, started building the Buck Lake Club cabin in 1962 with the help of brothers-in-law Joseph O. and Erwin Yancey and friends. It took them nearly three

Buck Lake Club camp

Photo by Andy Flynn

years and 5,000 hours to complete. It rested on a bluff overlooking Buck Pond (the Virklers called it Buck Lake). The northern shoreline is now in the Watson's East Triangle Wild Forest, and the western, southern and eastern shoreline is in the Pepperbox Wilderness Area.

The Buck Lake Club cabin, a real-deal Adirondack hunting camp, is now an exhibit at the Adirondack Museum. There are many items inside the camp from the Virkler family, including blankets, bedrolls, frying pans, plates, kettles, a cutting board and fireplace tools. Other items were donated by Scott Chartier, Thomas Donnelly, Diane Brush and Laura Rice. Even one of Clarence Petty's rifles is on display. The one-room interior includes two bunks, a fireplace, tables, shelving, gas lighting fixtures, a sink and front and back doors. The front porch includes a bench. And green insulators on the outside logs are reminders of the homemade electric fence/shield that Virkler strung around the cabin to keep the bears out.

The fireplace was built with stones Virkler had collected over the years: garnet, rose quartz, flint, obsidian, agate, tourmaline and magnetite. The family kept many of the semiprecious stones.

Michael Carleton Virkler was born in Castorland, graduated from high school in 1923, and graduated in 1927 from Hamilton College, where he studied languages (German, French, Latin, Italian and Spanish) and geology. During World War II, he served in the U.S. Army, and he spent 30 years selling fuel oil. He owned a 191-acre certified tree farm, took snow-depth measurements for the DEC at Buck Pond, helped with searches and rescues, and was a licensed guide. He wore many hats, but, above all, Virkler was a woodsman who respected the forest and its many creatures. And in the fall, he was a hunter who liked to go up to camp, spend time with his family and friends, and enjoy the hunt for a trophy buck.

(This story was first published in Andy Flynn's book, "New York State's Mountain Heritage: Adirondack Attic, Volume 5.")

Adirondack Forest Preserve Units

- Aldrich Pond Wild Forest (St. Lawrence)
- Black River Wild Forest (Hamilton, Herkimer, Oneida)
- Blue Mountain Wild Forest (Hamilton, Essex)
- Blue Ridge Wilderness Area (Hamilton)
- Camp Santanoni Historic Area (Essex)
- Chazy Highlands Wild Forest (Clinton, Franklin)
- Cranberry Lake Wild Forest (St. Lawrence)
- Crown Point Historic Area (Essex)
- Debar Mountain Wild Forest (Franklin)
- Deer River Primitive Area (Franklin)
- Dix Mountain Wilderness Area (Essex)
- Ferris Lake Wild Forest (Fulton, Hamilton)
- Five Ponds Wilderness Area (Herkimer, St. Lawrence)
- Fulton Chain Wild Forest (Herkimer)
- Giant Mountain Wilderness Area (Essex)
- Gore Mountain Ski Center (Warren)
- Grasse River Wild Forest (St. Lawrence)
- Ha-De-Ron-Dah Wilderness Area (Herkimer)
- Hammond Pond Wild Forest (Essex, Warren)
- High Peaks Wilderness Area (Essex, Franklin, Hamilton)
- Hoffman Notch Wilderness (Essex)
- Horseshoe Lake Wild Forest (Franklin, St. Lawrence)
- Hudson Gorge Primitive Area (Essex, Hamilton)
- Hurricane Mountain Fire Tower Historic Area (Essex)
- Hurricane Mountain Wilderness Area (Essex)
- Independence River Wild Forest (Herkimer, Lewis)
- Jay Mountain Wilderness Area (Essex)
- Jessup River Wild Forest (Hamilton)
- Lake Champlain Islands Complex (Clinton, Essex)
- Lake George Wild Forest (Warren, Washington)
- Little Moose Mountain Wilderness (Hamilton)
- Lows Lake Primitive Area (St. Lawrence)
- Madawaska Flow-Quebec Brook Primitive Area (Franklin)
- Moose River Plains Wild Forest (Hamilton, Herkimer)
- Pepperbox Wilderness Area (Herkimer)
- Pharaoh Lake Wilderness Area (Essex, Warren)
- Pigeon Lake Wilderness Area (Hamilton, Herkimer)
- Raquette-Jordan Boreal Primitive Area (St. Lawrence)
- Raquette River Wild Forest (St. Lawrence)
- Round Lake Wilderness (Hamilton, St. Lawrence)
- St. Regis Canoe Area (Franklin)
- St. Regis Mountain Fire Tower Historic Area (Franklin)
- Saranac Lakes Wild Forest (Essex, Franklin)
- Sargent Ponds Wild Forest (Hamilton)
- Sentinel Range Wilderness Area (Essex)
- Shaker Mountain Wild Forest (Fulton, Hamilton)
- Siamese Ponds Wilderness Area (Hamilton, Warren)
- Silver Lake Wilderness Area (Hamilton)
- Split Rock Mountain Wild Forest (Essex)
- Taylor Pond Wild Forest (Clinton, Essex, Franklin)
- Vanderwhacker Mountain Wild Forest (Essex, Hamilton, Warren)
- Watson's East Triangle Wild Forest (Herkimer, Lewis)
- West Canada Lakes Wilderness (Hamilton, Herkimer)
- West Canada Mountain Primitive Area (Herkimer)
- White Hill Wild Forest (St. Lawrence)
- Wilcox Lake Wild Forest (Fulton, Hamilton, Saratoga, Warren)
- William C. Whitney Wilderness Area (Hamilton)
- Wilmington Wild Forest (Clinton, Essex)

Wild about the Park

What thinks like a weasel, moves like a cat, and dines on porcupine?

An Adirondack riddle: meet the fisher (who prefer meat to fish). European settlers thought they were polecats, so the name comes from *fichet*, French for polecat pelt.

Kissing cousins to the ermine, mink and pine marten, fishers have Canadian relatives, but call the Adirondack Park home.

Fishers actually prefer dining on soft, fuzzy snowshoe hare over crunchy porcupine (but quills make nice toothpicks).

Though 19th century hunters and trappers nearly made fishers extinct, conservation is now helping their numbers. Bad news for the bunnies.

Find out more: contact AdirondackCouncil.org

Wild things happen in the Adirondacks.

ADIRONDACK COUNCIL
www.AdirondackCouncil.org

INTERNATIONAL (A) PAPER
www.internationalpaper.com

Natural History Illustration by Sheri Amsel   www.exploringnature.org

Principles for Forest Preserve Use

Know the Park

Know about the Adirondack Park and understand that it is a 6-million-acre patchwork of public and private lands. Choose places appropriate for your activities and abilities.

•The 2.5 million acres of public land within the Adirondack Park are protected by the New York State Constitution, is known as the Forest Preserve and is made up of different land classifications. Specific rules and regulations determine what types of activities are permitted on the different types of Forest Preserve land classifications.

Protect Yourself

Have the proper clothing and equipment to protect yourself and the environment.

•When venturing outdoors, the proper clothing and equipment can mean the difference between life and death, will help lighten your impact on the land, and will help keep you comfortable.

Know where you are going, have a map, stay on trails or have the advanced navigational skills necessary for off-trail travel.

•Know where you are, and keep your group together on the trails and waterways. Good travel technique involves good group organization, conserving energy and safe maneuvering over varied terrain.

Maintain health through adequate hydration, balanced diet, good hygiene and knowledge of first aid.

•Food and water keeps us warm, helps us fight illness, allows the body to maintain itself properly and helps us to keep a positive attitude. Good hygiene helps prevent wound infections and avoid stomach illness caused by food spoilage, poor food handling and waste contamination.

Protect the Park

Plan ahead and prepare to assure safe, enjoyable and environmentally sound outdoor travel.

•Match your physical ability, your available clothing and equipment and other planning factors to the level of difficulty and remoteness of your intended excursion.

Travel and camp on durable surfaces to protect the environment.

•Utilize existing trails and established campsites or use special care in camping and hiking in pristine areas.

Dispose of waste properly, including human, food and packaging waste.

•Correctly disposing of human waste helps prevent pollution of water sources, the spread of illness such as giardia, and limits unpleasant aesthetic impacts to other visitors. Human waste should be disposed in outhouses, cat holes or latrines. All food waste and packaging should be packed out.

Leave what you find. Preserve natural and cultural heritage by leaving cultural and natural objects where you find them.

•People come to the Adirondacks to enjoy it in its natural state. Allow others the same sense of discovery by leaving plants, rocks and artifacts as you find them.

Minimize campfire impacts to leave the outdoors looking natural.

•Campfires can cause lasting impacts. Only set fires where they are allowed. Employ best campfire practices by keeping them small, using only downed wood and setting fires in designated campsite fire rings or appropriate "mineral soil" sites.

Respect wildlife, and be aware of wildlife and their habitat for your safety and theirs.
•Protect wildlife and yourself by not feeding or approaching animals and safely securing your food and food waste away from all wildlife. Take precautions and protect yourself responsibly against insects and vector-borne diseases such as Lyme disease and the West Nile virus.

Be considerate of other visitors so they may also enjoy the outdoors.
•Respecting other visitors means avoiding loud noises and voices, keeping pets under control and obeying all New York state rules and regulations. Recognize that all legal forms of recreation have their place and everyone deserves to be treated with courtesy.

The Adirondacks on Horseback
DEC STAFF

Before you go, here are a few tips.

Know where you are going.
•Obtain and study maps of the area.
•Familiarize yourself with the trails and terrain.
•Research parking area sizes to make sure your rig will fit.
•Check to see if mounting blocks and hitching rails are available.

Prepare your horse.
•Check your horse's shoes to make sure they are tight.
•Ensure your horse is conditioned for rugged terrain.
•Bring insect repellent for yourself and horse.
•Rabies shot and negative coggins are required.

Carry and use proper equipment.
•Use of safety helmet is strongly recommended.
•Pack a first-aid kit with the basics for you and your horse.
•Weather can be changeable; prepare for rain or cold.
•Carry a cell phone on you, not your horse; that way, if you part company with your horse, you have the phone.

Act properly on the trail.
•Ride on designated horse trails only.
•Sign in at trail registers.
•Slow horses to a walk if you meet other users (hikers, bikers, etc.).
•Ask people to speak to you and your horse. Horses have different eyesight and may not recognize people with packs or on bikes as people.
•Do not tie horses to live trees.
•Be prepared to encounter wildlife: deer, bear, turkeys, grouse, etc.

Henry Van Hoevenberg Hat

ANDY FLYNN

We don't necessarily remember Henry Van Hoevenberg (1849-1918), "the man in leather," for his fashion sense, yet his legacy remains as durable as his favorite fabric. As the builder of the original Adirondack Lodge near Lake Placid, he was a pioneer in hospitality, outdoor recreation and so much more.

Let's start with one of his hats, which is on display at the Adirondack Museum. A brown, leather peak cap hangs against a sky blue wall in the mountain climbing case. Several historic photographs of Van Hoevenberg, known affectionately as Mr. Van, show him wearing a hat like this one. It looks as though this could be the cap Mr. Van held on the ground as he sat against a white pine tree on page 64 of "The Finest Square Mile: Mount Jo and Heart Lake," by Sandra Weber. The cap was donated by the Lake Placid Club.

Van Hoevenberg was born on March 22, 1849 in Oswego, and he grew up in Troy, according to Weber. He was a successful telegraph operator and inventor before traveling to the Adirondack Mountains for the first time in 1877. That two-week camping trip to Upper Ausable Lake in Essex County would change his life forever. He and a party of friends, including the legendary "Josephine Scofield," climbed Mount Marcy. Together they picked out a site for their future home in the wilderness, the "finest square mile" around Clear Lake, known today as Heart Lake. Van Hoevenberg named the nearby mountain after her, Mount Jo.

In her book, Weber dispelled the myth of "Josephine" and identified the real woman, Miss Jane (Jennie) J. Scofield, of Woodstock, Ontario.

"It seems she used the name Josephine or Jo while in the Adirondacks," Weber wrote. "Presumably her middle initial J. stood for Josephine, although there is no document to certify it ... perhaps it was her pen name."

It is no mystery what happened next. Although her body was never found, Scofield apparently committed suicide by jumping over Niagara Falls on Oct. 15, 1877. Filled with grief, Van Hoevenberg continued his plans to build a home in the Adirondacks, and, in 1878, he purchased 640 acres around Clear Lake, including Mount Jo. That's where he built the first Adirondack Lodge, known at the time as "the greatest log structure in the whole world," according to Godfrey Dewey, who wrote an obituary tribute to his close friend in the March 1, 1918 issue of the Lake Placid News.

During construction of the Adirondack Lodge in 1878 and 1879, Van Hoevenberg found that he needed durable clothing in order to roam through the wilderness in search of wood for his world-class log hotel.

Henry Van Hoevenberg leather hat
Photo courtesy of the Adirondack Museum

"The rustic work used so skillfully and lavishly inside and out was selected only by painstaking search of large areas of untouched forest," Dewey wrote. "It was after wearing out a corduroy suit every week or so ... that Mr. Van first conceived the idea of his leather clothing."

Van Hoevenberg bought calfskin and buckskin clothing, "softer than broadcloth and wearing like iron, through 20 years and more of hard service," Dewey wrote. As we already know, he also wore leather hats.

The two years of construction would yield

Henry Van Hoevenberg

Photo courtesy of the Adirondack Museum

an array of Adirondack tales, penned by Van Hoevenberg for the benefit of his future guests. After the Adirondack Lodge opened in 1880, this larger-than-life figure would spin these yarns around the campfire, mesmerizing visitors and adding to the legend of Mr. Van, the man in leather.

Hiking excursions from the 50 miles of wilderness trails radiating from Clear Lake would further enhance his reputation. Many of the trails that he opened are still being used today by visitors to the High Peaks Wilderness Area and the Adirondack Mountain Club's Adirondak Loj. One is aptly named the Van Hoevenberg Trail.

In the mid 1890s, Van Hoevenberg lost control of the Adirondack Lodge and surrounding property and in the late 1890s moved to the Lake Placid Club, a growing resort on the shore of Mirror Lake, where he became postmaster and a telegraph operator. In 1900, the Lake Placid Club purchased the Adirondack Lodge, and Van Hoevenberg returned to the log hotel as the manager and host. Clear Lake was soon re-named Heart Lake, as there was already a Lake Clear in nearby Franklin County. Mr. Van wouldn't stay there for long. Tragedy struck in 1903 when the Adirondack Lodge was destroyed by a forest fire.

Van Hoevenberg moved back to the Lake Placid Club after the fire. Although the resort wouldn't construct a new Adirondak Loj until 1927, it built open camps along some of the old trails in the early 1910s. Mr. Van was named the first president of the resort's Adirondack Camp and Trail Club in 1910. In 1917, he moved out of the Lake Placid Club to expand his business, the Adirondack Electric Co. On Feb. 17, 1918, he suffered an attack of angina pectoris and was moved to the Lake Placid Club, where he died on Feb. 25.

The Adirondack Mountain Club (ADK) began leasing the Adirondak Loj from the Lake Placid Club in 1932 and bought the property in 1958. ADK continues to offer world-class hospitality and outdoor recreational opportunities at Heart Lake with the Loj, the High Peaks Information Center and a campground. It is the largest trailhead in the Adirondack Park, with trails leading to Keene Valley, Newcomb and the highest peaks in New York state.

(This story was first published in Andy Flynn's book, "New York State's Mountain Heritage: Adirondack Attic, Volume 4.")

Dogs and the Forest Preserve

DEC STAFF

Dog owners should act responsibly and always ensure that their dogs are under the control for the safety of the dog and wildlife and to allow an enjoyable outdoor experience for other recreational users.

Never let your dog out of your sight and always be capable of controlling them through voice command or physical restraint, such as a leash.

•Dogs may be injured by wildlife that is defending itself or its young.

•Wildlife diseases such as rabies and distemper may be transmitted to dogs during physical contact.

•Dogs can stress, injure or kill wildlife, especially young ones.

•Wildlife that is chased, or otherwise harassed, by dogs can use energy reserves that they need to survive long, harsh Adirondack winters.

•Not all people in the outdoors like dogs; some are intimidated or frightened by dogs.

•Even those people who like dogs don't appreciate being jumped on by a dog, especially one with wet or muddy paws.

•In the Eastern High Peak Wilderness, dogs must be maintained on a leash on trails, at primitive tent sites, at lean-to sites, at elevations above 4,000 feet, or at other areas where the public congregates.

•Hunters recreate on state lands and won't appreciate dogs frightening off game they are pursuing.

•Trapping regulations prohibit the setting of traps within 100 feet of a trail, except in Wildlife Management Areas. Regulations also restrict the size of body-gripping traps set on land and require that these type traps be set in a way that prevents the capture of dogs and other non-target animals. However, dogs that wander more than 100 feet from a trail run the risk of being caught in a leg-hold trap. This won't cause serious injury to the dog; however, it will restrain them at a location and make it difficult for owners to find them.

•Dogs in a leg-hold trap could spend up to 48 hours exposed to the elements during the fall and winter.

Enjoy your time in the outdoors with your dog, but take steps to protect your dog, protect the wildlife and respect other outdoor recreationists.

Lou Lou at Middle Saranac Lake, Franklin County

Photo by Andy Flynn

Leave Young Wildlife Alone

DEC STAFF

If You Care, Leave it There.

Spring is the peak season for giving birth or hatching young wildlife. It is not uncommon to find a fawn, bird or other young wildlife by itself. People should keep their distance and not disturb them.

Do not disturb fawns and other young wildlife.

Many people assume that young wildlife found alone are abandoned, helpless and need assistance for their survival. In nearly all cases this is a mistake, and typically human interaction does more damage than good. If you see a fawn or other newborn wildlife, enjoy your encounter, but for the sake of their well being, it is important to keep it brief and maintain some distance.

Young wildlife quickly venture into the world on shaky legs or fragile wings. While most are learning survival from one or both parents, some normally receive little or no parental care. Often, wild animal parents stay away from their young when people are near. For all of these young animals, the perils of survival are a natural part of life in the wild. Some will not survive. However, young wildlife that learn these important survival skills are the most fit and usually live the longest.

White-tailed deer fawns present a good example of how human intervention with young wildlife can be problematic. Most fawns are born during late May and early June. While fawns are able to walk shortly after birth, they spend most of their first several days lying still. During this period a fawn is also usually left alone by its mother except when nursing. People do occasionally find a lone fawn and mistakenly assume it has been orphaned or abandoned, which is very rare. In such a case, fawns should not be picked up. In fact, if human presence is detected by the doe, the doe will delay its next visit to nurse. Human scent can also put the fawn at risk by attracting predators to the site.

A fawn's best chance to survive lies in being raised by its mother. Fawns nurse three to four times a day, usually for less than 30 minutes at a time, but otherwise the doe keeps her distance. This helps reduce the chances that she will attract a predator to the fawn. The fawn's protective coloration, near lack of scent and ability to remain motionless all help it avoid detection by predators and people.

By the end of its second week, a fawn begins to move about more and spend more time with its mother. It also begins to eat grass and leaves. At about 10 weeks of age, fawns are no longer dependent on milk, although they continue to nurse occasionally into the fall. During August, all deer begin to grow their winter coat and fawns lose their spots during this process.

Should you find a fawn or other young wildlife, always remember: "If You Care, Leave it There." It may be difficult to do, but this is the real act of kindness and in nearly all cases that is the best thing to do. DO NOT consider young wildlife as possible pets. This is illegal and harmful to the animal. Wild animals do not make good pets; they are not well suited for life in captivity and they may carry diseases that can be given to people. Resist the temptation to take them out of the wild.

For more information and answers to frequently asked questions about young wildlife, visit the DEC website at http://www.dec.ny.gov/animals/6956.html.

This bear in downtown Long Lake was eating apples and garbage in September 2012 before a state Department of Environmental Conservation staffer shot and killed it. Residents had been feeding this 90-pound female yearling, and it was deemed a nuisance after becoming dependent on humans and getting too close to children. If you care, don't feed the bears.

Photo by Christine LaRocque

Black Bears in the Adirondacks

DEC STAFF

Wild, non-habituated black bears forage for foods such as berries, nuts, insects, and grasses. These bears will not normally show an interest in our food unless they are first introduced to it through our careless behavior. Remember the following.

1) Feeding bears is bad for bears.

2) A fed bear is a dead bear.

3) It is illegal to feed bears.

It's simple. Keep our Adirondack bears wild by keeping all of your food and garbage sealed up tight. Below are some bear tips for your Adirondack trip.

At the campground

• Never leave food, garbage, coolers or dirty dishes unattended at your campsite.

• Store food and garbage in your car and out of site. Keep the windows shut and food and coolers out of sight.

• Use a food storage unit where provided, such as food lockers.

• Clean up immediately after meals. Keep pots and pans, grills, cooking utensils and washbasins clean after each use. Do not wash dishes under the water faucets.

• Do not place food scraps, grease, garbage, diapers, cans, bottles or other garbage in the fireplace. Burning food scraps makes the smell more attractive to bears. The only thing that should go into the fireplace is fuel for the fire and even that should only be put in the fireplace while you have a fire. Never put waste in the fire.

• Keep your campsite clean. Take all garbage and recyclables to the recycling center daily.

• Never bring any food, garbage, coolers or odorous item in your tent, including toothpaste, soaps and candy wrappers.

In the backcountry

• Keep a clean, organized camp. Food and garbage odors can attract bears from a considerable distance.

• Make sure that you know where all of your food is and store it properly and a safe distance from your camp.

• Use a commercially manufactured bear-resistant food canister to store your food, toiletries, and garbage. Canisters are required in the Eastern High Peaks Wilderness Area and are a proven effective means for preventing bears from obtaining your food. Consider using bear-resistant food canisters on all of your trips. The can be purchased or rented from many outdoor equipment retailers and outfitters.

• Learn about the natural, seasonal bear foods in your camping area and try to avoid disturbing areas where they may be feeding.

At camp or home

• Store garbage securely indoors, not on a porch, or use bear-resistant garbage cans.

• Do not burn garbage. Burning garbage makes it more attractive to bears and is illegal in many communities.

• Clean up any odorous scraps or items from your yard or lakefront area such as fish carcasses, grease, fat or dirty diapers.

• If you have garbage pickup service, put garbage at the curb the morning of pick up, not the night before.

• Keep barbecue grills clean and free from grease. Turn them on high for a few minutes after cooking. Keep them inside, if possible.

• Bird feeders are a strong attractant for bears, even if they cannot reach it. Feed the birds in the winter months only.

• Do not feed family pets outside. An empty dish can attract a bear.

Feeding the Bears Photo

ANDY FLYNN

Once upon a time, when we had landfills operating in the Adirondacks, watching hungry black bears parade down a roadway in the evening was a fairly predictable occurrence. Now, black bear sightings are not as common, and they are left to chance. Yet New York State Department of Environmental Conservation (DEC) officials are still trying to reduce the number of bear-human interactions, which mainly occur when the bears are searching for food.

It used to be a common evening activity for Adirondack families — drive down to the local dump and watch the bears. Not only watch them but feed them. This was such a popular tradition among residents that visitors soon caught on, and bear watching became a tourist attraction, an activity they would remember for years. And they had to get pictures, climbing out of their cars and walking several feet away from the bears with snouts and tongues poking through open car windows, grabbing at the freshly purchased local fare.

The food was certainly fresher than anything the bears could find in the landfill. It was literally dessert, marshmallows mostly. Marshmallows were great because the bears loved the sweetness, so you know they'd come to your car. And marshmallows are small and portable; they were perfect projectiles for throwing out a car window rolled almost to the top.

I remember feeding the bears with my family soon after we moved to Tupper Lake in 1976 when I was 6 years old. We drove toward Long Lake on Route 30, exited at the Bog River Falls road, and parked behind a line of cars on the road between the veterans' camp on Big Tupper Lake and Horseshoe Pond. There was a dump off the road, and bears congregated just before dusk to feed. It was predictable, and it was fun. It also looked dangerous, as many people got out of their vehicles to feed the bears and take photos.

One person who braved the bears in the open air and lived to tell the tale was Tupper Lake photographer Kathleen Bigrow, who took photos for the local newspapers. One of her photographs is in the Adirondack Museum's Historic Photo Collection.

Dating to the 1960s, this photo shows a black bear standing with its paws against a car door, with his snout inches away from a barely-open passenger-side car window. The bear is ready to grab food that a person in the car is poking through the window opening. A man and woman are standing directly behind the car, maybe 5 feet away from the bear, watching. Several feet behind them, a man leans toward the bear to snap a photograph. Two other cars are parked in a line in front of this vehicle. A driver of one car is standing outside with the door open.

This was a common scene in the Adirondacks before the state forced the closure of all the municipal solid waste landfills inside the Park's Blue Line. The DEC was in charge of landfill closures, which was a statewide initiative. On Sept. 17, 1984, the DEC commissioner issued an enforcement directive titled, "Closure of Active Solid Waste Landfills." It was revised on Dec. 29, 1988. The object was to help clean up the environment by closing unlined landfills throughout the state. Closing and capping landfills in the Adirondacks was the norm in the 1990s.

Between 1984 and 1994 the number of active landfills in New York state was reduced from more than 500 to about 50, according to the DEC. As of 2012, there were 26 active municipal solid waste landfills — none in the Adirondack Park.

Bears, however, continue to be a nuisance because they continue to be hungry. In their search for food, particularly during dry summers, bear-human interactions increase. The stories are endless. A bear breaks into a Blue Mountain Lake convenience store and eats

This photo was captured by Kathleen Bigrow in the 1960s near Tupper Lake.

Photo courtesy of the Adirondack Museum

most of the ice cream in the freezer. A bear breaks into a Paul Smiths home while the owners are on the West Coast and leaves the place wrecked and the cats scared half to death. Campers at Marcy Dam have their tent shredded by a bear because they left food inside. Hungry bears maul garbage cans throughout the Adirondack Park. These are all true stories. Almost everyone has a bear story to tell.

The DEC has taken steps to curb bear-human interactions in the backcountry and in communities, offering tips for homeowners and campers on its website. On Aug. 24, 2005, the DEC mandated that campers use bear canisters in the Eastern High Peaks Wilderness Area from April 1 to Nov. 30. The traditional "bear bags" don't work anymore in places like Marcy Dam and Lake Colden. The bears there have adapted and learned how to get any food hanging in a bag, but they can't get into the plastic bear canisters, yet. The DEC offers bear canister information sheets on its website.

In the fall, we go from feeding bears to feeding on bears. By mid-September, it's bear-hunting season in the Adirondacks. In 2012, Early Bear was from Sept. 15 to Oct. 12; Bowhunting was from Sept. 27 to Oct. 19; Muzzleloading was from Oct. 13 to Oct. 19; and Regular Bear was from Oct. 20 to Dec. 2.

In 2011, 1,258 bears were "harvested" in New York state (up from 1,064 in 2010): 275 in the Adirondack State Park (down from 521 in 2010), 353 in the Allegany State Park (up from 142 in 2010), and 630 in the Catskill State Park (up from 401 in 2010).

"Bear harvest rates in the Adirondacks typically drop in the early season during years of abundant soft mast (cherries, raspberries and apples), while the take will increase during the regular season in years with abundant beech nuts," states the DEC. "Beech nut abundance was mixed throughout the Adirondacks (in 2011) and the regular season bear take was approximately 15 percent below the five-year average."

(This story was first published in Andy Flynn's book, "New York State's Mountain Heritage: Adirondack Attic, Volume 5.")

Technology in the Backcountry

DEC STAFF

Technology has made it safer to recreate in the Adirondacks, allowing people to take bigger risks, knowing — or thinking — that the technology provides a safety net. Three electronic devices have had some of the biggest effects on backcountry recreation — the cell phone, GPS and personal locator devices.

Cell phone benefits

•During emergencies, such as lost or injured people, situational information can be reported quickly and completely, ensuring a timely and proper response by forest rangers.

•Lost persons can communicate directly with searchers allowing them to find them easier or direct them out of the woods.

•Cell phones with GPS can be used by 911 operators to provide coordinates of caller to DEC dispatch.

Cell phone weaknesses

•Service in the Adirondacks is spotty and undependable!

•While mountain tops are better, not all of them have service.

•911 calls can end up in Vermont or other distant locations.

•Batteries cannot be recharged in the backcountry.

•Accuracy of GPS varies according to satellite coverage at the time.

•Recreationists too often rely on the phone as a safety net — instead of proper planning and preparation.

•Use for other than emergency situations can ruin the backcountry experience.

GPS device benefits

•These devices can store a lot of information in a small amount of space as well as providing real time information such as location.

•It's a useful device for planning trips (present location and determining progress).

GPS device weaknesses

•Signals may be weak or non-existent under dense tree cover.

•Designed to be less than 100 percent accurate and accuracy varies according to satellite coverage.

•It is somewhat complicated to learn. The user must be sure to fully understand how the device works before entering the woods.

•It must be properly calibrated and have the correct maps loaded before a trip.

•Batteries cannot be recharged in the backcountry.

•A topographic map and compass are significantly less expensive and more dependable.

Personal locator device benefits

•Efforts to find the user can be initiated by just by pushing a button. You don't need to communicate by voice with someone.

•Able to pinpoint your location accurately, depending on the model.

•Some devices allow you to communicate your location, progress and condition — allowing people to contact emergency personnel if necessary with relevant information.

Personal locator device weaknesses

•Responders have no information on the specifics of a user's situation — must assume emergency medical care is needed and send significant resources.

•Signal sent to "call centers" in other parts of the country that may not contact the correct emergency response agency (i.e. DEC forest rangers).

•Due to ease of use, it can be accidentally set off.

•If used in non-emergency circumstances, the user can be subject to prosecution.

Invasive Species and You

HILARY SMITH

You have the gear. You have the perfect weather. But do you have a hitchhiker, too? The "nature" of travel and outdoor recreation has changed. Human activities aid the spread of invasive species when plants and pests hitchhike with us to new areas. Seeds and plant fragments can cling to our boats, boots, or bikes, and critters can be contained within bait buckets or firewood, to name a few pathways. Citizens are now taking measures to prevent the spread of invasive species by making inspection and cleaning part of the sport.

Invasive species are plants, animals and other organisms that cause environmental and economic harm. Introduced to areas outside of their native range, invasive species have no natural predators to keep their populations in check. They spread uncontrollably and can cause irreversible damage. Invading plants clog waterways. Non-native forest pests can kill trees. Invasive fish can destroy fisheries.

Help keep woods and waters free of invasive species. Follow these simple steps to save the Adirondacks from harm.

Protect rivers and streams.

Paddlers and anglers: Inspect, clean and dry all waders, gear and equipment before moving between waterways. Didymo, or "rock snot," is a microscopic algae that is easily spread on the bottoms of felt-soled waders or other damp items that come into contact with water.

Keep forests safe.

Hikers and campers: Use firewood local to the area you are visiting. Forest pests like emerald ash borer and Asian longhorn beetle hitch rides in firewood and cause the loss of millions of trees.

Guard lakes and ponds.

Boaters and anglers: Inspect, clean, and dry all gear and equipment, motorboats and trailers, canoes and kayaks before moving between waterways. Fragments from invasive plants like Eurasian watermilfoil and seeds from water chestnut are easily spread on boat props and trailer carpets. Invasive invertebrates like spiny waterflea can be transported on fishing tackle and bait buckets.

Defend natural areas.

Gardeners and Homeowners: Landscape with only non-invasive plants. Many plants stay put, but some plants like Oriental bittersweet, yellow iris and purple loosestrife escape gardens and invade neighboring woods, wetlands and waters.

Please take these precautions to help protect the fisheries and forests of the Adirondacks. Learn more ways to prevent the spread of invasive species online at www.adkinvasives.com; www.protectyourwaters.net; www.dontmovefirewood.org; and www.beplantwise.org.

You CAN make a difference. If not you, then who?

(Hilary Smith is the director of the Adirondack Park Invasive Plant Program, a partnership program housed at the Adirondack Chapter of the Nature Conservancy in Keene Valley, N.Y.)

Parkwide Organizations

The **Adirondack Association of Towns and Villages, Inc.** acts as a representative of the towns and villages of the Adirondacks in addressing issues unique to local government and residents within the Adirondack Park. The organization works to develop a consensus on the resolution of Adirondack issues. Main office: Mayfield, (518) 661-7622. Web: http://aatvny.org.

The **Adirondack Council** is a not-for-profit environmental group that has been working since 1975 to protect the open-space resources of the Adirondack Park and to help sustain the natural and human communities of the region. Its mission is "to ensure the ecological integrity and wild character of the Adirondack Park for current and future generations." Its vision is "an Adirondack Park with clean air and water and large wilderness areas, surrounded by working farms and forests and vibrant local communities." Main office: 103 Hand Ave., Suite 3, Elizabethtown, (877) 873-2240. Communication and Legislative office: Albany, (518) 432-1770. Web: www.adirondackcouncil.org.

The **Adirondack Economic Development Corporation (AEDC)** was established in 1984 to coordinate economic development activities for the 14-county North Country region. The AEDC offers classroom training for small businesses and is a U.S. Small Business Administration certified lender and microloan intermediary. The AEDC's Business Resource Center provides links to information of interest to business owners on topics including Customer Service, Marketing, Management and Technology. Office: 67 Main St., Saranac Lake, (518) 891-5523. Web: www.aedconline.com.

The **Adirondack Mountain Club (ADK)**, founded in 1922, is a nonprofit membership organization that protects wild lands and waters through a balanced approach of conservation and advocacy, environmental education and responsible recreation. ADK's mission is to represent all those who love wild places and to ensure that those places are protected and accessible for generations to come. ADK has chapters all over New York state and operates two lodging facilities in the Adirondack Park, Johns Brook Lodge (a 3.5-mile hike from Keene Valley) and the Adirondak Loj/High Peaks Information Center 8 miles south of Lake Placid at the end of the Adirondack Loj Road. Headquarters: 814 Goggins Road, Lake George, (518) 668-4447. Public Affairs office: Albany, (518) 449-3870. Web: www.adk.org.

The **Nature Conservancy**, a leading international non-profit organization working to protect ecologically important lands and waters for nature and people, has been working in the Adirondacks since 1971. You may recognize some of the places this group has helped to conserve, such as Lake Lila, Santanoni Preserve, and Lyon Mountain, which are all public lands available to everyone for recreation and respite. The Adirondack Land Trust, established in 1984, protects working farms and forests, undeveloped shoreline, scenic vistas and other lands contributing to the quality of life in the Adirondacks. Together, these partners in Adirondack conservation have protected more than 571,000 acres. Office: Keene Valley, (518) 576-2082. Web: www.nature.org/adirondacks.

The **Adirondack North Country Association (ANCA)**, founded in 1954, is a non-profit private corporation that strengthens the economy and quality of life in the 14 counties of northern New York through informed, open debate and advocacy on economic issues critical to the region. ANCA provides regionwide services and programs in enterprise and community development, working landscapes, capacity building, culture and tourism. Office: Saranac Lake, (518) 891-6200. Web: www.adirondack.org.

The **Adirondack Park Invasive Plant Program** is a cooperative effort initiated in 1998 among citizens and organizations of the with a mission to protect the Adirondack Park region from the negative impacts of nonnative invasive species. The program coordinates two projects: the Aquatic Invasive Species Project and the Terrestrial Invasive Species Project. Office: Route 73, Keene Valley, (518) 576-2082. Web: www.adkinvasives.com.

The **Adirondack Park Local Government Review Board** consists of members appointed by the governing bodies of the 12 counties wholly or partly in the Adirondack Park. Board members work to insure that the interests of the people of the Adirondack Park and their local governments are protected as the Adirondack Park Agency carries out its duties set forth in the Adirondack Park Agency Act (Executive Law Sections 801-810). Executive Director: Frederick H. Monroe, Chestertown. Phone: (518) 494-3607. Web: www.adkreviewboard.com.

The mission of **Adirondack Wild: Friends of the Forest Preserve** is to advance New York's "Forever Wild" legacy and Forest Preserve policies in the Adirondack and Catskill parks, and promote public and private land stewardship that is consistent with wild land values through education, advocacy and research. Paul Schaefer (1908-1996) founded Friends of the Forest Preserve in 1945. Senior Partner/Chair: Peter Brinkley. Mailing Address: PO Box 9247, Niskayuna, NY 12309. Web: www.adirondackwild.org.

Protect the Adirondacks! (PROTECT) is a non-profit, grassroots membership organization dedicated to the protection and stewardship of the Adirondack Park's public and private lands, and to building the health and diversity of its human communities and economies for the benefit of current and future generations. PROTECT results from a 2009 consolidation of the Residents' Committee to Protect the Adirondacks and The Association for the Protection of the Adirondacks. General contact: PO Box 769, Lake George, NY 12845, (518) 685-3088. Executive Director: Peter Bauer. Web: www.protectadks.org.

The **Wildlife Conservation Society**, with an office at 7 Brandy Brook Lane, Saranac Lake, promotes wildlife conservation and healthy communities in the Adirondacks through applied research, community partnerships and public outreach. The WCS scientists are studying population trends of common loons, moose and boreal birds to implement informed conservation measures. They are also investigating the impact of different types of land use on wildlife and ecologically sensitive areas, identifying land-use recommendations, and providing tools and guidelines to help communities and land managers ensure that development is environmentally sound. Phone: (518) 891-8872. Web: www.wcs.org.

The Adirondack Mountain Club, based in Lake George, operates two lodges — the Adirondak Loj above near Lake Placid and the Johns Brook Lodge near Keene Valley — and has chapters throughout New York state. The Adirondak Loj trailhead is the largest in the Adirondack Park and is a gateway to popular High Peaks Wilderness Area destinations such as Mount Marcy and Algonquin Peak, the highest and second-highest peaks in the state at 5,344 and 5,114 feet above sea level, respectively.

Photo by Andy Flynn

1856 Clinton County Map

ANDY FLYNN

The 1856 wall map of Clinton County, published by O.J. Lamb in Philadelphia, Pa., is like a storybook. It tells about life in the northeastern corner of New York state, bordering Canada to the north, Lake Champlain and Vermont to the east and the great Adirondack wilderness to the south and west.

Time stands still in this snapshot of pre-Civil War America.

I knew I would write about this map the minute it was sprawled in front of me in June 2005 in the Adirondack Museum's library. Taking a break from my day's research, I scanned the yellowish brown map with Librarian Jerry Pepper. Covering the entire table, it showed obvious signs of age: cracking paper and darkening varnish. Yet it was complete, and it was decorated with different colors around the town boundary lines. The museum already owns an original black-and-white copy of the same map, but it had been clipped around the edges and cut in half horizontally, discarding important cartography and illustrations around the border.

This wall map is a gem. It was made from surveys by A. Ligowsky and helps illustrate the iron mining and iron processing industries in Clinton County. Villages are well established at ports on Lake Champlain and at strategic hydropower points along rivers such as the Ausable. The map shows railroads beginning to penetrate the North Country, forming railroad towns around depots. It is the age of horses, and many buildings on the map support this crucial form of transportation in the mid 19th century.

The 1856 Clinton County map, which would have been used in schools or government offices, shows all 13 townships: Ausable, Beekmantown, Black Brook, Champlain, Chazy, Clinton, Dannemora, Ellenburg, Mooers, Plattsburgh, Peru, Saranac and Schuyler Falls. The town of Dannemora had just been founded in 1854, so this was an up-to-date document. Yet the map only had a shelf life of one year before it became outdated. A 14th township, Altona, was formed in 1857 from the western part of Chazy.

While many of the property owners are named on rural areas of the map, even more details are provided in separate maps of the larger villages around the border. Illustrations and census data are also printed in this border section. For example, one drawing depicts the Northern R.R. Station at Rouses Point, and another shows Saranac Falls.

The 1855 census information explains that there were 42,634 residents in Clinton County, compared to 82,128 in 2010. The town of Champlain was the most populated in 1855 with 6,204 people, and the town of Dannemora was the least populated with 726.

Some place names have changed over the years. The hamlet/tourist attraction we know as Ausable Chasm on the "Great Au Sable River" was Birmingham Falls, complete with a wool factory, a starch factory, a papermill, a schoolhouse and a blacksmith shop. A bend in the Ausable River between Au Sable Forks and Clintonville was a hamlet in 1856 called New Sweden, featuring a forge, a sawmill, two schoolhouses and a store on the northern Clinton County shore, a bridge across the river to Essex County, and a forge and a separator on the southern shoreline.

The detailed village maps are tasty globs of eye candy to history junkies like me. And the most impressive villages were Au Sable Forks and Keeseville.

In 1856, Au Sable Forks was home to Rogers Powen & Co., manufacturer of iron nails and lumber, where the forks of the east and west branches of the Ausable River joined and created the Great Au Sable River. The village had two nail factories, two forges, a foundry, two sawmills, a rolling mill, a tannery, two schoolhouses, a post office, a gristmill and Catholic and Methodist churches.

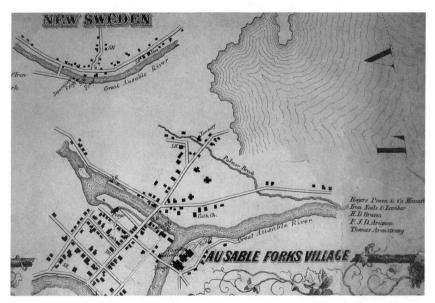

A detailed map of Au Sable Forks on the 1856 Clinton County map

Photo courtesy of the Adirondack Museum

Keeseville, on the Great Au Sable River, was home to two nail factories, a foundry, two machine shops, a rolling mill, a chair factory, a planing and stave factory, a sawmill, a grist-mill, a schoolhouse and churches (Irish Catholic, Baptist, Episcopal, Methodist, etc.).

Clintonville on the Great Au Sable River had two forges, a foundry, a nail factory, a sawmill, a ballasthouse, a schoolhouse, a separator and Presbyterian and Methodist churches.

The hamlet of Black Brook had a sawmill and a forge, and it was home to "Rogers Martin & Com., Manfct. of Iron & Lumber." A large iron mine was east of the community at Palmer Hill, and settlements radiated to the north, south and west. A blacksmith shop, the Comestock Tavern and a coal kiln were located on the road northwest to Sampson Pond and Union Falls.

Cadyville had two taverns, a forge, a blacksmith shop, a schoolhouse, a sawmill and a post office. A plank road from the east went through Cadyville westward to the hamlet of Elsinore and northwestward to the community of Dannemora.

Clinton State Prison in Dannemora opened in June 1845 and is known today as the max-imum-security Clinton Correctional Facility. Dannemora inmates were used to mine iron ore, and the 1856 map shows buildings in and around the state-funded operation: a store-house, a steam sawmill, a separator, coal kilns, a foundry, a forge, a schoolhouse, a black-smith shop, the "state mine," a machine shop, a store and a post office.

There are many more hamlets, villages and points of interest on this map — Redford, Saranac, Rouses Point, Port Gilliland, Port Jackson, the city of Plattsburgh, a Quaker com-munity at The Union, etc. — all with great stories about their past. Yet my space is limited. Anyone interested in seeing old maps should contact local historical societies and research rooms such as the Adirondack Museum library. Be forewarned, though, scanning through these documents can be addicting.

(This story was first published in Andy Flynn's book, "New York State's Mountain Her-itage: Adirondack Attic, Volume 3.")

Adirondack Counties Map

County Government

Clinton County: The Clinton County Government Center is located at 137 Margaret St., Plattsburgh, NY 12901. County clerk: (518) 565-4700. Web: www.clintoncountygov.com.

Essex County: The Essex County Government Center is located at 7559 Court St., Elizabethtown, NY 12932. County clerk: (518) 873-3600. Web: www.co.essex.ny.us.

Franklin County: The Franklin County Government Center is located at 355 West Main St., Malone, NY 12953. County clerk: (518) 481-1681. Web: http://franklincony.org.

Fulton County: The Fulton County Government Center is located at 223 West Main St., Johnstown, NY 12095. County clerk: (518) 736-5555. Web: www.fultoncountyny.gov.

Hamilton County: The Hamilton County Office Building is located on Route 8, Lake Pleasant, NY 12108. County clerk: (518) 548-7111. Web: www.hamiltoncounty.com.

Herkimer County: The Herkimer County Government Center is located at 109 Mary St., Herkimer, NY 13350. County clerk: (315) 867-1129. Web: http://herkimercounty.org.

Lewis County: The Lewis County Government Center is located at 7660 North State St., Lowville, NY 13367. County clerk: (315) 376-5333. Web: http://lewiscountyny.org.

Oneida County: The Oneida County Office Building is located at 800 Park Ave., Utica, NY 13501. County clerk: (315) 798-5794. Web: http://ocgov.net.

St. Lawrence County: The St. Lawrence County Government Center is located at 48 Court St., Canton, NY 13617. County clerk: (315) 379-2237. Web: www.co.st-lawrence.ny.us.

Saratoga County: The Saratoga County Government Center is located at 40 McMaster St., Ballston Spa, NY 12020. County clerk: (518) 885-2213. Web: www.saratogacountyny.gov.

Warren County: The Warren County Municipal Center is located at 1340 State Route 9, Lake George, NY 12845. County clerk: (518) 761-6427. Web: www.co.warren.ny.us.

Washington County: The Washington County Municipal Center is located at 383 Broadway, Fort Edward, NY 12828. County clerk: (518) 746-2170. Web: www.co.washington.ny.us.

Essex County Government Center, Elizabethtown

Photo by Andy Flynn

Towns, Villages and Hamlets

The following counties, towns, villages and hamlets are located wholly or partially within the 6-million-acre Adirondack Park. Only two of the 12 counties included in this list are completely within the Park's boundaries: Essex and Hamilton. We did not include cities, towns, villages or hamlets from counties that are not located inside the Park.

Clinton County (County Seat: Plattsburgh)
•Town of Altona, (518) 236-7035
•Town of Ausable (village of Keeseville and hamlets: Clintonville, Harkness), (518) 834-9052 (town of Ausable), (518) 834-9059 (village of Keeseville)
•Town of Black Brook (hamlet of Au Sable Forks), (518) 647-5411
•Town of Dannemora (village of Dannemora and hamlet of Lyon Mountain), (518) 492-7541 (town), (518) 492-7000 (village)
•Town of Ellenburg (hamlets of Ellenburg Center, Merrill), (518) 594-7507
•Town of Peru (hamlet of Peasleeville), (518) 643-2745
•Town of Plattsburgh, (518) 562-6800
•Town of Saranac (hamlets of Redford, Saranac, Standish), (518) 293-6666

Essex County (County Seat: Elizabethtown)
•Town of Chesterfield (village of Keeseville and hamlets of Ausable Chasm, Port Kent), (518) 834-9042 (town), (518) 834-9059 (village of Keeseville)
•Town of Crown Point (hamlets of Crown Point, Ironville), (518) 597-3235
•Town of Elizabethtown (hamlets of Elizabethtown, New Russia), (518) 873-6555
•Town of Essex (hamlet of Essex), (518) 963-4287
•Town of Jay (hamlets of Au Sable Forks, Jay, Upper Jay), (518) 647-2204
•Town of Keene (hamlets of Keene, Keene Valley), (518) 576-4444
•Town of Lewis (hamlet of Lewis), (518) 873-6777
•Town of Minerva (hamlets of Minerva, Olmstedville), (518) 251-2869
•Town of Moriah (village of Port Henry and hamlets of Mineville, Moriah, Moriah Center, Witherbee), (518) 546-8631 (town of Moriah), (518) 546-9933 (village of Port Henry)
•Town of Newcomb (hamlet of Newcomb), (518) 582-3211
•Town of North Elba (villages of Lake Placid and Saranac Lake, and hamlet of Ray Brook), (518) 523-9516 (town of North Elba), (518) 523-2597 (village of Lake Placid), (518) 891-4150 (village of Saranac Lake)
•Town of North Hudson (hamlet of North Hudson), (518) 532-9811
•Town of St. Armand (hamlet of Bloomingdale), (518) 891-3189
•Town of Schroon (hamlets of Paradox, Schroon Lake, Severance), (518) 532-7737
•Town of Ticonderoga (hamlet of Ticonderoga), (518) 585-6677
•Town of Westport (hamlets of Wadhams, Westport), (518) 962-4419
•Town of Willsboro (hamlet of Willsboro), (518) 963-8668
•Town of Wilmington (hamlet of Wilmington), (518) 946-7174

Franklin County (County Seat: Malone)
•Town of Bellmont (hamlets of Brainardsville, Mountain View, Owls Head), (518) 483-2728
•Town of Brighton (hamlets of Gabriels, Paul Smiths, Rainbow Lake), (518) 327-3202
•Town of Duane (hamlet of Duane Center), (518) 483-1617
•Town of Franklin (hamlets of Loon Lake, Onchiota, Vermontville). (518) 891-2189

The Ausable River splits the village of Keeseville in two, separating one side in the Essex County town of Chesterfield and the other side in the Clinton County town of Ausable. Above you can see the old nail factory on the left and the historic 1843 Stone Arch Bridge.

Photo by Andy Flynn

Theaters like the Strand here in the Herkimer County hamlet of Old Forge are still the pride of their communities. In 2013, the Strand and other theaters in the Adirondack Region collaborated on a "Go Digital or Go Dark" fundraising campaign with the Adirondack North Country Association to make the conversion from film projectors to digital.

Photo by Andy Flynn

•Town of Harrietstown (village of Saranac Lake and hamlet of Lake Clear), (518) 891-1470 (town of Harrietstown), (518) 891-4150 (village of Saranac Lake)
•Town of Santa Clara (hamlet of Santa Clara), (518) 891-7190
•Town of Tupper Lake (village of Tupper Lake), (518) 359-9261 (town), (518) 359-3341 (village)
•Town of Waverly (hamlet of St. Regis Falls), (518) 856-9482

Fulton County (County Seat: Gloversville)
•Town of Bleecker (hamlet of Bleecker), (518) 725-8382
•Town of Broadalbin (hamlets of North Broadalbin, Union Mills), (518) 883-4657
•Town of Caroga (hamlet of Caroga Lake), (518) 835-4211
•Town of Ephratah (hamlet of Rockwood), (518) 762-5688
•Town of Johnstown, (518) 762-7070
•Town of Mayfield (village of Mayfield), (518) 661-5414 (town), (518) 661-5165 (village)
•Town of Northampton (village of Northville), (518) 863-4040 (town of Northampton), (518) 863-4211 (village of Northville)
•Town of Oppenheim, (518) 568-2837
•Town of Stratford (hamlet of Stratford), (315) 429-8612

Hamilton County (County Seat: Lake Pleasant)
•Town of Arietta (hamlet of Piseco), (518) 548-3415
•Town of Benson, (518) 863-4969
•Town of Hope, (518) 924-3821
•Town of Indian Lake (hamlets of Blue Mountain Lake, Indian Lake, Sabael), (518) 648-5885
•Town of Inlet (hamlet of Inlet), (315) 357-5771
•Town of Lake Pleasant (village of Speculator and hamlet of Lake Pleasant), (518) 548-3625 (town of Lake Pleasant), (518) 548-7354 (village of Speculator)
•Town of Long Lake (hamlets of Long Lake, Raquette Lake), (518) 624-5441
•Town of Morehouse (hamlets of Hoffmeister, Morehouse), (315) 826-7744
•Town of Wells (hamlet of Wells), (518) 924-7912

Herkimer County (County Seat: Herkimer)
•Town of Ohio (hamlets of Atwell, North Wilmurt, Ohio), (315) 826-7912
•Town of Russia (hamlet of Grant), (315) 826-3432
•Town of Salisbury, (315) 429-8581
•Town of Webb (hamlets of Beaver River, Big Moose, Eagle Bay, Old Forge, Stillwater, Thendara), (315) 369-3121

Lewis County (County Seat: Lowville)
•Town of Croghan, (315) 346-1212
•Town of Diana, (315) 543-0030
•Town of Greig (hamlet of Brantingham), (315) 348-8859
•Town of Lyonsdale, (315) 348-8249
•Town of Watson, (315) 221-1945
Oneida County (County Seat: Utica)
•Town of Forestport (hamlets of Otter Lake, Woodgate), (315) 392-2801
•Town of Remsen, (315) 831-5558

St. Lawrence County (County Seat: Canton)
•Town of Clare, (315) 386-3084
•Town of Clifton (hamlets of Cranberry Lake, Newton Falls, Star Lake), (315) 848-2915
•Town of Colton, (315) 262-2810
•Town of Fine (hamlets of Fine, Oswegatchie, Star Lake, Wanakena), (315) 848-3121
•Town of Hopkinton (hamlets of Hopkinton, Nicholville), (315) 328-4187
•Town of Parishville, (315) 265-6180
•Town of Piercefield (hamlets of Childwold, Conifer, Piercefield), (518) 359-7544
•Town of Pitcairn, (315) 543-2111
Saratoga County (County Seat: Ballston Spa)
•Town of Corinth (village of Corinth), (518) 654-9232 (town), (518) 654-2012 (village)
•Town of Day, (hamlet of Day Center), (518) 696-3789
•Town of Edinburg (hamlets of Batchellerville and Edinburg), (518) 863-2034
•Town of Greenfield, (518) 893-7432
•Town of Providence, (518) 882-6541

Warren County (County Seat: Queensbury)
•Town of Bolton (hamlet of Bolton Landing), (518) 644-2444
•Town of Chester (hamlets of Chestertown, Pottersville, Riparius The Glen), (518) 494-2711
•Town of Hadley (hamlet of Hadley), (518) 696-4797
•Town of Hague (hamlets of Graphite, Hague, Silver Bay), (518) 543-6161
•Town of Horicon (hamlets of Adirondack, Brant Lake), (518) 494-3647
•Town of Johnsburg (hamlets of Bakers Mills, Johnsburg, North Creek, North River, Wevertown), (518) 251-2421
•Town of Lake George (village of Lake George and hamlet of Diamond Point), (518) 668-5722 (town of Lake George), (518) 668-5771 (village of Lake George)
•Town of Lake Luzerne (hamlet of Lake Luzerne), (518) 696-2711
•Town of Queensbury (hamlets of Assembly Point, Cleverdale, Katskill Bay), (518) 761-8200
•Town of Stony Creek (hamlet of Stony Creek), (518) 696-3575
•Town of Thurman (hamlets of Athol, Thurman), (518) 623-9649
•Town of Warrensburg (hamlet of Warrensburg), (518) 623-4561

Washington County (County Seat: Fort Edward)
•Town of Fort Ann, (518) 639-8929
•Town of Dresden (hamlets of Huletts Landing, Clemons, Dresden Station), (518) 499-1813
•Town of Putnam (hamlet of Putnam Station), (518) 547-8317

Tim Fortune Photomosaic

ANDY FLYNN

An Adirondack artist embarks on an inner quest of creativity for himself and his hometown, taking almost 3,000 1-inch-square photos of his village – people, places, animals – and creating a mosaic of himself, a 4-by-5-foot self-portrait made with images of family, friends and strangers. The title of the artwork: "It Takes a Village to Raise an Artist."

This project has had a profound impact on the artist and the community. The impact, however, won't be fully realized until time has a chance to chew on it for a while. History will be the ultimate art critic.

The village was Saranac Lake. The artist, Tim Fortune. The year, 2000.

"We are shaped through the years by bits and pieces of input like pixels in an electronic image," Fortune wrote after completing his self-portrait. "This input helps to shape our personalities in direct, as well as subtle, ways. A seed may be planted by a teacher. A peer group alters our sensitivity toward others. We become our parents."

A native Adirondacker, Fortune earned a bachelor's degree from Temple University's Tyler School of Art and a master's degree from New York University, and he studied art in Italy. In 1989, he returned home to Saranac Lake and opened his first studio, which features oil and watercolor landscape paintings. A decade later, Fortune opened a second gallery, where he exhibits "a photographic contemporary approach" to the Adirondack landscape.

In March 2000, Fortune began working on "It Takes a Village to Raise an Artist" by asking Saranac Lake residents to help him with this labor-intensive art project, and the response was overwhelming. Community members donated 2,820 photographs of themselves, their families, their pets, their homes and their workplaces. Even tourists donated photos.

Some pictures had dark backgrounds, some had light ones. Fortune used these shades to sculpt his face on a 5-foot-tall, 4-foot-wide piece of foam core mounted to plywood. He used white glue adhesive to attach the photos. He accepted black-and-white photos but preferred color.

Fortune started with the darker photographs, creating the outline of his face, his eyeglasses, hair, shirt, and the outline of a doorway behind him. Lighter photographs filled in the background, his shirt collar, and the softer tones of his face and neck. The mosaic blends the artist and community as one.

"The individual faces fade as in a melting pot, and a single identity emerges, just as I melt into the larger identity of my community and am a product of it," Fortune wrote. "In this work I am investigating the cumulative identities of my community and how they have contributed to defining my own identity."

This art project was made possible, in part, by a $2,500 ACE Grant from the New York State Council on the Arts Decentralization Program, administered locally by the Arts Council for the Northern Adirondacks in Westport.

As photographs began arriving at The Small Fortune Studio on Main Street in Saranac Lake, Fortune clipped them into 1-inch-square pieces. He also received photos at the Blue Moon Café on Main Street, where people could find him working on the mosaic most weekday mornings for the first four months.

"By encouraging participation in and witnessing of the progress of the mosaic, the people of the community exchanged ideas concerning the work while enjoying the process of discovery," Fortune wrote in his project description. "As the artist, I was available to talk with the people and explain the creative process."

The photos include group shots and head shots, buildings around town, bare backs, cats and dogs. You can't fully appreciate this art without getting close to it.

This 5-foot-tall, 4-foot-wide self-portrait mosaic of Saranac Lake artist Tim Fortune was made with 2,820 1-inch-square photographs.

Photo by Andy Flynn

Fortune collected photos for about 10 months and completed the project within a year. The Blue Moon Café unveiled the mosaic at noon on Sunday, April 1, 2001. He was also invited to display the artwork and share his "artistic vision and sense of community" with staff and students at Clinton Community College in Plattsburgh and at the SUNY College at Potsdam.

Although the Blue Moon Café played an important role in the creation of Fortune's mosaic, its display there was only temporary. Fortune sought a permanent home for "It Takes a Village to Raise an Artist," a place "where future generations can see the spirit of our Adirondack community and understand how our identities are formed by where we live."

In March 2003, Fortune's mosaic found a home at the Adirondack Museum in Blue Mountain Lake.

The artistic planning is over, the funding all spent, the creativity packaged and delivered. There's no more to do right now but wait. As the mosaic's real-life faces and places fade with time, history is born, the aging process begins. Luckily, we don't have to uncork this masterpiece to enjoy it. While in storage or on display, we'll always know that 2000 was an excellent year for art in the Adirondack village of Saranac Lake.

(This story was first published in Andy Flynn's book, New York State's Mountain Heritage: Adirondack Attic, Volume 3.*)*

Barienger Brakes Used in Logging

ANDY FLYNN

A century ago, lumber companies found challenging circumstances when it came to harvesting timber on the steepest Adirondack peaks, where grades became dangerous or impossible for horse teams to travel. Ingenuity prevailed, and companies came up with creative ways of getting their logs from the stump to the mill. One such innovation was the Barienger Brake.

The Adirondack Museum owns two Barienger Brakes that were donated by the Johnston Pulp Corporation, of the Lewis County hamlet of Port Leyden, in 1957. John E. Johnston was the chief contact at the Johnston Pulp Corporation. Port Leyden is strategically located on the Black River just a few miles south of where the Moose River empties into the Black River at the community of Lyons Falls, which has a rich history of papermaking mills. The Moose River originates from the wilds of the Adirondack Park, with branches around the Old Forge region, and flows westward outside the Blue Line.

Both Barienger Brakes are on display. The brake with four drums is located outside the building that houses the "Work in the Woods: Logging in the Adirondacks" exhibit. A smaller brake with two drums is displayed inside the building.

Barienger Brakes feature one or two pairs of cylindrical, grooved drums that look like stacks of pancakes on top of a sled. The catalog record for the four-drum brake describes it as "a vehicle consisting of ten foot seven inch long sled runners with a flat iron body on which are mounted four vertical drums, 25 inch diameter with grooved sheaves around which is wound a steel cable to haul or lower loaded sleds of logs. Two levers in rear control the drums in pairs of two."

The four-drum sled is 10-foot, 7 inches long and 2-foot, 9 inches wide. It was placed on top of white marble chip and was connected to a 17-foot-long sled of logs to show how the brake was used. The brake was restored under the direction of Bud Hayes in 1988, and the log sled was restored in 2005. Both were part of the Johnston donation.

The exhibit sign explains how the Barienger Brakes worked. They used 5/8-inch or 3/4-inch cable, which was connected from the brake drums to the back of the sled to ease the load down a hill, "keeping it from overtaking the horses." The brake was anchored to a sturdy stump at the top of the hill.

For the most part, lumber companies relied on the weight of a heavy load to cause enough friction between the sled runners and the logging road to slow down a sled. That didn't always work, according to the exhibit, especially in hilly terrain:

"If roads were icy and a sled got running too fast, the driver jumped to safety and the horses were left to race the sled to the bottom of the hill."

After lumberjacks chopped or sawed down their softwood trees, the logs were skidded to the skidways and piled up. Heavy-duty logging sleds were then used to transport logs from the skidways to the banking grounds, located either on lake or pond ice or adjacent to rivers. Logs were piled up on the banking grounds so they could be "let loose" in the springtime for the famed Adirondack river drives to the lumber or pulp and paper mills.

Work in the woods was dangerous, and logging accidents led to injuries and deaths in the Adirondacks. In 1925, a load of logs ran over 38-year-old lumberjack William Mertesky 20 miles north of Kildare in Franklin County, according to the Feb. 12, 1925 issue of the Adirondack Record-Elizabethtown Post. Mertesky was working on a hardwood job for the Oval Wood Dish Corporation, sanding an ice road on a hill. A team of horses was unhitched from the sled at the top of the hill and soon began sliding down toward Mertesky:

"It rapidly gained speed in its noiseless flight and before the unfortunate lumberjack knew

A logging crew uses a Barienger Brake.

Photo courtesy of the Adirondack Museum

what happened, he was struck. The sled ran over his body, mangling him in a terrible manner."

Lumberjacks carried Mertesky 20 miles through the snow on a logging road to the hamlet of Kildare. From there, he was driven to the hospital in Tupper Lake. The fact that he was still alive amazed doctors. Three ribs had punctured one of his lungs, and his collarbone and other bones were broken.

Working in the high peaks of the Adirondacks around the Cold River region was especially dangerous and difficult. The Santa Clara Lumber Company, based in Tupper Lake, harvested tracts around the Seward Range. But getting their logs from the peaks to the Cold River — where they were driven in the spring to the Raquette River and then to the company's mill on Raquette Pond in Tupper Lake — posed a greater challenge. The company installed two innovations around Mount Seward: the Barienger Brake and the "Slide." The Sept. 30, 1981 issue of the Tupper Lake Free Press published a story about a scrapbook that detailed the inner workings of logging operations around Tupper Lake, describing the Slide as "a heavy timber trough, greased and constructed to cradle long strings of logs, fastened end-to-end, which a team of horses could easily move down-grade."

The Feb. 13, 1914 issue of the Tupper Lake Herald reported that the Santa Clara Lumber Company was using a "novelty" to harvest its timber from the slopes of Mount Seward: a cable and steam engine as a substitute for horses." The cable lowered the loaded sleds down the mountain. Barienger Brakes helped the Santa Clara Lumber Company get 5 million feet of lumber from the Mount Seward tract to its mill in the spring of 1914.

(This story was first published in Andy Flynn's Adirondack Attic newspaper column in 2009.)

Transportation

The **Adirondack Regional Airport** is located in Lake Clear, Franklin County. **Cape Air** offers scheduled passenger service to Boston (www.flycapeair.com or call (800) 352-0714).

Adirondack Trailways offers scheduled bus service from Albany to these communities: Lake George, Warrensburg, Chestertown, Pottersville, Schroon Lake, Keene Valley, Lake Placid and Saranac Lake. Phone: (800) 776-7548. Web: www.trailwaysny.com.

Amtrak: The Adirondack travels daily from New York City to Montreal with stops in Plattsburgh, Port Kent, Westport, Port Henry and Ticonderoga. Book online at www.amtrak.com.

The **Lake Champlain Transportation Company** operates ferry service on Lake Champlain between New York and Vermont. The Northern Crossing (open year-round, weekends only in winter) is between Plattsburgh, N.Y. and Grand Isle, Vt. The Central Crossing (open May-October) is between Port Kent and Burlington. The Southern Crossing (open year-round) is between Essex, N.Y. and Charlotte, Vt. Phone: (802) 864-9804. Web: www.ferries.com.

Clinton County Public Transit serves Clinton County with seven countywide routes, including stops at Au Sable Forks, Keeseville, Ausable Chasm and Port Henry. Phone: (518) 565-4713. Web: www.clintoncountypublictransit.com.

Essex County Public Transportation offers scheduled bus service on three routes: Champlain Northern route (Elizabethtown, Essex, Willsboro), Champlain Southern Route (Elizabethtown, Westport, Moriah, Crown Point, Ticonderoga), and Mountain Valley Shuttle (Lake Placid, Wilmington, Jay, Ausable Forks). Phone: (518) 873-3886. Web: www.co.essex.ny.us.

Franklin County Public Transportation provides schdeuled bus service on several routes from Malone to Lake Placid, with stops at Paul Smiths, Tupper Lake and Saranac Lake. Phone: (518) 481-1598. Web: http://franklincony.org.

Placid XPRESS is a free shuttle service in Lake Placid. Signs around town indicate pick-up points. Phone: (518) 523-2445, x601.

The **Saratoga & North Creek Railway** offers daily passenger service Memorial Day weekend to Oct. 31 from Saratoga Springs to North Creek. Phone: (877) 726-7245. Web: www.sncrr.com.

Saratoga & North Creek Railway at the North Creek train station, Warren County
Photo by Andy Flynn

Ferry on Lake Champlain, Ticonderoga, Essex County

Photo by Andy Flynn

Gore Mountain shuttle bus for skiers, North Creek, Warren County

Photo by Andy Flynn

Pullman Car: The Oriental

ANDY FLYNN

What may seem out of place at the Adirondack Museum — a private car from the Louisville & Nashville Railroad that was never in service inside the Blue Line — is not out of place at all. This car, manufactured by the Pullman Company in the late 1800s, is typical of the cars found at train stations throughout the Adirondacks in the late 19th and early 20th centuries. They carried America's wealthiest families to resorts and retreats in this vast wilderness region.

By 1955, Adirondack Museum founder Harold Hochschild had secured the donation of the Marion River Carry Railroad's steam engine and one of its passenger cars for the Adirondack Historical Association's (AHA) artifact collection in Blue Mountain Lake. The opening of the museum was still two years away, and Hochschild, the AHA president, was extremely busy. In the midst of this period, he set out to find historical objects that would help tell the story of the Adirondack Park and its people, both residents and visitors. Given the remoteness of the mountains, transportation—from horses to railroads to automobiles—is a large part of that story and figured into his planning process.

"Raquette Lake region during the first fifteen years of this century was, as you probably had heard, remarkable for the concentration of extremely wealthy families who had summer camps here," Hochschild wrote in an April 4, 1955 letter to Charles W. Bryan Jr., president of the Pullman-Standard Car Manufacturing Company in Chicago. Hochschild, chairman of the Board of Directors of The American Metal Company, Ltd., of New York City, sent this correspondence on company letterhead. "The members of some of these families almost invariably made their visits to Raquette Lake in private railroad cars and it has been suggested to us that the association of private cars with Raquette Lake is sufficiently strong to warrant our trying to get hold of one as a permanent exhibit."

Indeed, the Raquette Lake area was teeming with wealthy Great Camp owners, such as the Vanderbilts, Carnegies, Morgans, Whitneys, Colliers and Huntingtons. The sidings at Raquette Lake station temporarily housed private cars such as Collis P. Huntington's Genesta, William C. Whitney's Wanderer, Alfred G. Vanderbilt's Wayfarer, R.J. Collier's Vagabondia, and Anthony N. Brady's Adventurer. These cars made their way on the New York Central & Hudson River Railroad mainly from New York City to Albany and Utica, then on the New York Central's Adirondack Division from Utica to Clearwater Station (later named Carter), and finally on the 18-mile Raquette Lake Railway (opening to public traffic in 1900) to Raquette Lake.

Hochschild found his private car, the Oriental, which was acquired from the Louisville & Nashville Railroad. It was built by the Pullman Company in 1889-90 for Long Island Railroad President Austin Corbin (1827-1896). It was named after one of Corbin's lavish resorts, the Oriental Hotel at Coney Island in Brooklyn, and was one of about 250 private cars made by the Pullman Company in the late 19th and early 20th centuries. At the time, Corbin was also the president of the Elmira, Cortland & Northern Railroad. His office was in Philadelphia, his residential mansion was in Manhattan, and his weekend/summer estate was in Babylon, Long Island. He certainly traveled comfortably in style on the Oriental.

The 69-foot-long car was constructed of 17,087 feet of framing lumber, 6,900 feet of mahogany and white mahogany, and yellow pine flooring. Two washstands were made of onyx, and the other was made of Tennessee marble. There was oil and electrical lighting and a great many ornate embellishments. It was finished in November 1890.

There is no evidence that Corbin ever traveled to the Adirondacks on the Oriental. However, he was one of the early members of the Adirondack Club (incorporated in 1877), orig-

The Pullman car Oriental is on display at the Adirondack Museum

Photo by Andy Flynn

inally called the Preston Ponds Club (1876) and later re-named the Tahawus Club (1898). This club in the town of Newcomb was formed in Manhattan by wealthy sportsmen.

On June 4, 1896, while visiting his home state of New Hampshire, Corbin was killed when his open carriage overturned. He was en route to a fishing expedition.

On March 30, 1897, less than a year after Corbin's death, the private car was sold to the Louisville & Nashville Railroad for use by its chairman, August Belmont Jr. (1853-1924), who was based in New York City. Belmont was the co-founder of the Belmont Park racetrack in Elmont, N.Y. and reportedly used his private railroad car, re-named the Louisville, to visit the race tracks in Saratoga Springs.

In 1903, the Louisville & Nashville Railroad's newest chairman, Henry Walters (1848-1931), inherited the Louisville car. Walters was also based in New York City. After his death, the Louisville was then sent to Louisville, Ky. and placed in storage.

In 1933, the car was renovated and given an ordinary, insignificant name: "362." It was then used by the Louisville & Nashville's vice president and general manager, W.E. Smith.

Steel siding and air conditioning were added in 1947, and the car was painted blue with gold trim in 1948. In 1952, it was sent to the Birmingham Division of the Louisville & Nashville Railroad to be used as an office for the division's superintendent, F.W. Kirchner. It was in service there through 1957.

By 1955, the Louisville had been promised to the Adirondack Museum. It had been transported to Weehawken, N.J. by late January 1958 and was refurbished before making the trip to the Adirondacks, via Albany and Utica, reaching Tupper Lake on Feb. 6, 1958. The wheels were taken off the car, and the front and back ends were loaded on top of logging trucks for the 35-mile journey to the Adirondack Museum (March 5-10). Once at the museum, the wheels were put back on the car, and the artifact was placed on its own tracks. Later the building it currently sits in was constructed around the car.

(This story was first published in Andy Flynn's book, "New York State's Mountain Heritage: Adirondack Attic, Volume 4.")

Communications

The **Adirondack Almanack** is the Adirondack Explorer's online news journal that covers news, history, nature and various social issues about the Adirondack Park. Web: www.adirondackalmanack.com.

The **Adirondack Daily Enterprise** is published in Saranac Lake daily except Sunday. Web: www.adirondackdailyenterprise.com.

The **Adirondack Explorer**, in Saranac Lake, is a bimonthly news magazine covering the Park. Web: www.adirondackexplorer.org.

The **Adirondack Express**, based in Old Forge, is a weekly newspaper covering the Old Forge area. Web: http://adirondackexpress.com.

Based in the hamlet of Jay, **Adirondack Life** is a regional magazine covering the Adirondack Park. Web: www.adirondacklife.com.

Denton Publications, based in Elizabethtown, publishes a series of weekly newspapers in the Adirondack Park: the Adirondack Journal (Warrensburg), News Enterprise (North Creek), Times of Ti (Ticonderoga), Valley News (Elizabethtown), and North Countryman and The Burgh (Clinton County). Web: www.denpubs.com.

The **Hamilton County Express**, based in Speculator, is a weekly newspaper covering Hamilton County. Web: www.hamconews.com.

The **Lake Placid News**, established in 1905, is published weekly and is the hometown newspaper. Web: www.lakeplacidnews.com.

The **Lake George Mirror**, based in Bolton Landing, is published weekly from late May to mid October and monthly in the off season. Web: www.lakegeorgemirror.com.

The **Weekly Adirondack**, based in Old Forge, is a weekly newspaper that covers Old Forge, Inlet and Raquette Lake. Web: www.weeklyadk.com.

WSLP, 93.3-FM, located in Lake Placid, offers a blend of adult contemporary music from the 1970s to today. Web: www.wslpfm.com.

Mountain Communications Radio: Based in Saranac Lake, MCR operates the following radio stations: WNBZ 1240-AM, Saranac Lake; Y-106, WYZY 106.3-FM, Saranac Lake; WIRD 920-AM, Lake Placid; and ROCK 105, which simulcasts on WLPW 105.5-FM, Lake Placid, and WRGR 102.3-FM, Tupper Lake. Web: www.mtnradio.com, www.wnbz.com, www.theclassicrock105.com.

North Country Public Radio, based in Canton, serves the region. Frequencies are located throughout the Park. Web: www.ncpr.org.

NCPR Main Transmitters: WSLU 89.5-FM Canton; WXLU 88.1-FM Peru/Plattsburgh/Burlington; WSLZ 88.1-FM Cape Vincent; WXLS 88.3-FM Tupper Lake; WSLJ 88.9-FM Watertown; WXLD 89.7-FM Lowville; WXLG 89.9-FM North Creek; WSLL 90.5-FM Saranac Lake; WSLG 90.5-FM Gouverneur; WXLQ 90.5-FM Bristol, Vt.; WSLO 90.9-FM Malone; WXLH 91.3-FM Blue Mountain Lake; WXLB 91.7-FM Boonville; WXLL 91.7-FM Lake Placid

NCPR Translators: W204BJ 88.7-FM Old Forge; W211BU 90.1-FM Keene; W212BQ 90.3-FM Morristown; W206BH 89.1-FM Lyons Falls; W205BW 88.9-FM Paul Smiths; W217AE 91.3-FM Alexandria Bay; W219BG 91.7-FM Long Lake; W224BI 92.7-FM Wells; W228BO 93.5-FM Lake George; W237BR 95.3-FM Schroon Lake; W242AZ 96.3-FM Keene Valley; W247BB 97.3-FM Newcomb; W247BJ 97.3-FM Glens Falls; W248BL 97.5-FM Speculator; W262BO 100.3-FM Clayton; W269BR 101.7-FM St. Huberts; W271AW 102.1-FM Jay; W272BL 102.3-FM Carthage; W282AV 104.3-FM North Creek (village)

About the Author/Publisher

Andy Flynn is an author and publisher living in Saranac Lake , N.Y. In 2004, he founded Hungry Bear Publishing and published his first book, "New York State's Mountain Heritage: Adirondack Attic, Volume 1," and his catalog now includes six "Adirondack Attic" books and "Saranac Lake Winter Carnival Memories." His "Adirondack Attic" and "New York's Bluegrass Trail" radio shows air on North Country Public Radio.

For the "Adirondack Attic" material, Flynn works with curators at the Adirondack Museum in Blue Mountain Lake to tell human-interest stories about the facility's artifact collections. His weekly "Adirondack Attic" column ran in several newspapers from 2003 to 2009. In 2008, Flynn was awarded a Certificate of Commendation from the Upstate History Alliance for the Adirondack Attic History Project.

Flynn is currently the Assistant Managing Editor for Denton Publications in Elizabethtown, N.Y., where he also serves as Editor of the North Creek News Enterprise. He operates Hungry Bear Publishing with his wife, Dawn, publishing the "Adirondack Attic" book series and the Meet the Town community guides. From 2001 to 2009, he was employed as the Senior Public Information Specialist at the New York State Adirondack Park Agency Visitor Interpretive Center (VIC) in Paul Smiths and Newcomb.

Flynn is an award-winning journalist, garnering merits of excellence from the National Newspaper Association, New York Newspaper Publishers Association and the New York Press Association (NYPA) for photography, headline writing, editorial writing, news writing, feature writing, front-page layout and community service reporting. While the staff writer at the Lake Placid News, he was named the 1996 NYPA Writer of the Year for weekly New York state newspapers with circulations under 10,000.

Prior to the VIC, Flynn was a writer and managing editor for the Adirondack Daily Enterprise in Saranac Lake and the Lake Placid News, a correspondent for the Plattsburgh Press-Republican, an announcer for WNBZ 1240-AM in Saranac Lake, and a general assignment news reporter and radio documentary producer for North Country Public Radio.

Flynn earned a bachelor's degree in communication at the SUNY College at Fredonia in 1991 and graduated from the Tupper Lake High School in 1987.

He continues to work on writing projects to share the wonders of the Adirondack Region with the world. Learn more at www.hungrybearpublishing.com.

Andy Flynn at the Adirondack Museum, Blue Mountain Lake, Hamilton County

Emergency Contacts

General emergencies: Call 911

NYSDEC Dispatch

Phone Number: (877) 457-5680

The New York State Department of Environmental Conservation operates a dispatch center at the DEC Region 5 Office in Ray Brook to a 24 hours a day — 7 days a week operation, which has statewide responsibilities after regular business hours and on holidays.

The DEC Emergency Dispatch should only be contacted to report backcountry emergencies (lost or injured people and wildfires) or violations of Environmental Conservation Law and regulations.

When you call, remain calm, and provide as much information as possible, try to answer all the questions asked by the dispatchers. They are doing their best to ensure that the response is quick and proper. Do not call for directions or other information!

The **New York State Police** protects the Adirondack Park through three troops: Troop B, based in Ray Brook, (518) 897-2000, serves Clinton, Franklin, Essex, St. Lawrence and Hamilton counties; Troop D, based in Oneida, (315) 366-6000, covers Lewis, Herkimer and Oneida, counties; and Troop G, based in Loudonville, (518) 783-3211, serves Fulton, Hamilton, Saratoga, Warren and Washington counties. Web: http://troopers.ny.gov.

Report Environmental Problems (24 hours/day, confidential)

*1-800-TIPP DEC (1-800-847-7332) — call the TIPPs hotline to report any environmental violations

*1-800-457-7362 (within New York state) or (518) 457-7362 (outside New York state) — call the Spill Hotline to report a chemical or oil spill

*(518) 891-0235 — to report lost or injured hikers or a wildland fire

If a deer flies through your windshield, call the State Police. This eight-point buck hit the author's car in 2006 in Lake Placid and flew through the windshield of an oncoming car, landing in the passenger's seat. The pregnant woman driving the vehicle was treated and released with minor injuries at the hospital. The deer was given to the fire department.

Photo by Andy Flynn